zero

Stories & Essays
by Sarah Voss

zero

ISBN 0-940121-48-4
Library of Congress Catalog Card Number: 98-073466

Photos by Dan Sullivan

Published by Cross Cultural Publications, Inc.
PO Box 506
Notre Dame, Indiana 46556, U.S.A.
Phone: (219) 272-0889 • Fax (219) 273-5973

Cross Cultural Publications, Inc.
CrossRoads Books

Introduction to the Series

In this age of information overload, massive print distribution, and millennial uncertainty, thematic collections of short, inspirational essays have often captured the reading public's fancy. Certainly they have captured mine. So, as a minister to a church without walls, which is how I define my service as a Unitarian Universalist community minister, I decided to try my hand at authoring such a collection. What I wound up with was not one collection, but four: *Zero, One, Two,* and *Many.*

You will note a certain mathematical theme to these four books. That's because I like mathematics. In fact, I was a mathematics teacher before I entered the ministry. However, if mathematics isn't your thing, don't be alarmed. The mathematics in this series is mostly symbolic. The twenty-four pieces in *Zero*, for instance, all exemplify the notion of something from nothing. *One* is a collection of reflections about the meaning of unity. *Two* reflects the tension of opposites in contemporary life. *Many* captures the richness of everyday life when it is viewed through the qualitative device of being "too large to count."

All of the essays and stories in this series are easy reads, too, culled from real-life experiences and/or from what some might call an overactive imagination. Many of them began life as sermons. If sermons aren't your thing either, you still need not be alarmed. While the entire series joins the realm of "faith" literature, I avoid religious dogmas in favor of posing questions on relevant issues that affect the meaning and purpose, the heart and soul of the ordinary individual's life. At least I try to. My oldest daughter, Sonna, suggested that I'm too preachy in some of them, but I figure that's common for daughters about mothers. Still, after her observation I did go back and rework a few of them. You'll have to judge for yourselves.

Speaking of daughters, and sons and spouses as well, I want to acknowledge right up front my appreciation of my own immediate family for their steadfast support and help in bringing this series into being. Sonna and Melinda (daughters), Wil (son), and Dan (spouse) not only contributed time, effort, and professional skill to the actual production of the books, but they also graciously permitted me to use them as the focus of my message from time to time. You'll meet them all somewhere throughout the pages of this series. The pictures are Dan Sullivan originals; the graphic design and photo enhancement are Sonna and Wil's work, respectively. The suggestions that helped improve the final manuscripts are theirs, although not theirs entirely: in particular, Richard Thill, Flo Thill, Elisabeth Young, and my editor Cyriac Pullapilly all also offered invaluable advice. The credit is theirs. The gratitude is mine. The pleasure, I hope, is yours.

It is easy to form a chain from a string of zeros.
-Stanislaw Jerzy Lec

Black holes are where God divided by zero.
-Source unknown

About ZERO

Zero is a symbol for nothing.

for Sonna, who taught me to appreciate Nothing

Contents

Nothing

Nothing is not a topic to be lightly dismissed. Just exactly what is nothing? Do you have to be of a certain age, or a certain breed, to do nothing? What are some of the benefits of doing nothing? Who does nothing best? How can you tell when it's time to do it? Are there spiritual implications of nothing? These are the sorts of questions which this book addresses.

Nothing means no thing, the absence of thing. It differs substantially from some-thing, any-thing, every-thing. Yet, paradoxically, there is a distinct connection between the four notions. Nothing is the parent of something, any-thing, and everything. We can begin to grasp this family connection if we take a look at the history of our mathematical concept of "zero." Zero, to most of us, is the symbol of nothing. We can trace its etymological roots to the Latinized form *zephirum* of the Arabic word *sifr*. *Sifr,* in turn, is a derivation of the Hindu *sunya*, meaning *void*, or *empty*. On the other hand, when the word *sifr* first found its way into Germany in the 1200s, it was as *ciphra*, from which we obtain our present word *cipher*, meaning *code* or, more specifically, *the key to a code*. Thus, we may attribute to the term *zero* the concepts of both emptiness and somethingness; the nothingness of zero gave birth to the very "key" to de*cipher*ing, or "making out the meaning of."

Something from nothing is a concept familiar to most of us. In Genesis 1:2, we read that in the beginning "the earth was without form and void." Out of this void, this original nothingness, came the entire universe as we know it. In ancient times, Plato reasoned "that nonbeing must in some sense be, otherwise what is it that there is not?" Closer to our own day, John-Paul Sartre wrote that "man presents himself…as a being who causes nothingness to arise in the world," and Martin Heidegger ventured that "das Nichts nichtet" or "the nothing nothings."

The nothing nothings. The nothing annihilates. That's tricky. Yet the whole idea of nothing giving rise to *some*thing is tricky. Somehow it's easier to let nothing be nothing than to have it be something. The facts suggest, however, that we love nothing. We sing about it. "Nothing says something like something…." Or, "there is nothing like a dame…." We make song recordings of it. We write books about it. In one little library alone, I found almost one hundred seventy titles of songs and books which begin with the word "Nothing." Figuring a conservative average of $10 over-the-counter sales price per book or recording and, again conservatively, say 6000 sales of each, that's $10,200,000. That's quite a few coins to come out of such a tiny bit of nothing. And that's nothing when you compare it to what other folks have gotten out of nothing. Buddha, for example, thoroughly understood the importance of nothing—doing nothing is how you get enlightenment.

Surely we, too, should be able to appreciate the value of nothing, or at least of doing it. We do. We just don't practice it enough. We have work to do. We have jobs to handle, letters to write, kids to tend, cars to fix, bills to pay, floors to sweep, gifts to buy. The list goes on and on. Furthermore, we sometimes seem to have a built-in distrust of people who do nothing—particularly kids who do nothing. Kids, especially teens, are masters of the subtle meaning of nothing. After all, it's what they're always accused of doing. Once, my oldest daughter came home from college for a visit and announced that she was going to do nothing. This is every parent's nightmare—kids come home and do nothing forever. It's scary.

My daughter Sonna did nothing so well that vacation that I decided to do it, too. I filled the bath tub to the top with warm sudsy water and climbed in, firmly intending to laze away in endless bliss. Only I found I couldn't do it. In my head, I wrote a poem. Nothing gave birth to something! I still have the poem. It's called "Reflections on Doing Nothing":

Nothing tops doing nothing.
But if you're the addictive
sort—compulsive,
perfectionist, workaholic,
Type A, over achieving, over
dedicated, over zealous, doing
nothing is climbing Mt. Everest
with crippled feet
or flying an airplane
without any fuel
or stopping the rain
the day you planned
a garden party. Doing nothing
takes willpower and more
imagination than a three-hooved
hog hobbling into church.
Doing nothing requires a steel cold
glare when someone stalks
into the room where you are
doing nothing, smiles meaningfully,

and asks what are you doing?
And if that someone carries
an armload of groceries
or a sweeper or a rake
or an expectant expression,
doing nothing needs a weapon
more devastating than hot nuclear
fusion—needs the truth. Keep your
cold glare, if you wish, but
insist firmly, flatly, that you
are doing nothing and that you
are working hard at doing nothing
because, if you're not
careful, you will wind up
doing something and then
you will never
ever get nothing done.

I dedicated this poem to my daughter, who, bless her, fully appreciated it and took its meaning to heart.

Nothing is important and it's important to do nothing because nothingness nurtures the creative and the sacred in life. Everything comes from nothing. You are not yet convinced? Perhaps you think that doing nothing is really a very foolish idea. If so, you may be more correct than you realize.

For example, we find a very graphic depiction of the foolishness of doing nothing in the tradition of the Tarot, a tradition whose origins are attributed to the ancient Egyptians and/or to the Jewish Cabala. Among the Tarot cards we find the figure known as the Fool. A typical Fool is "a court jester with caps and bells and motley" or "a dreamer about to step over the precipice of the world." Liam Miller says of this Fool that his "countenance is full of intelligence and expectant dream. He has a rose in one hand and in the other a costly wand, from which depends over his right shoulder a wallet curiously embroidered. He is prince of the other world on his travels through this one…. He is everyman, born into the world 'not in entire forgetfulness,'…. He is…'the initial nothing' who must make his way to 'the terminal all,' the twenty-first key, called *The Universe*."[1]

In a Tarot deck, all cards are numbered, but the number on the Fool's card is zero. The Fool has become the Joker of our modern-day playing cards. Like the Joker, the Fool alone remains outside the pack, for he is the "Zero of the pack", the card which represents nothing. Paradoxically, however this

Zero card is also said to exert great power, for the Fool represents the "one who is the spirit in search of experience." Out of the Fool's nothingness is born his experience of the universe—is born, in other words, everything.

Out of *Zero*, All.

Evil

See no evil, speak no evil, hear no evil and, by all means, don't fool around. Of course, the world would be different if everyone followed this injunction. Imagine, if you can, a society with zero evil. Not heaven, although that may be the closest most of us can come to naming such a place. No, I'm talking ordinary society here. We all pay lip service to wanting such a society, but still I wonder....

Maxine was an evil-buster. Wherever Maxine went, evil just sort of busted apart, disappearing into thin air or wherever it is that evil goes when it's gone. Being an evil-buster wasn't something Maxine particularly tried to do. She was just a natural-born evil-buster—a peculiarity of nature with roughly one in ten million billion odds.

Now, on Planet Earth there have lived only a small fraction of ten million billion people, so most folks were surprised when an honest to goodness evil-buster was born to John and Dorina Brown on June 17th, 1999. That's a common fallacy among the mathematically naive, however. If the odds are one in ten million billion, many people assume that it takes precisely one more than 9,999,999 billion people before the odds "come true." But that reasoning is wrong. For instance, among the population at large the odds are roughly one in thirteen that an individual will be left-handed, yet that certainly doesn't mean that every thirteenth child is born left-handed. In fact, in certain families everyone is left-handed. In just that same way, an evil-buster can be born at any time. It is even possible that two evil-busters might be born one right after the other, although that is not how it happened with Maxine. Maxine Brown was the only evil-buster humankind had ever experienced, and, for that reason, she was generally considered something of a freak.

When Maxine, after an easy, virtually painless delivery, took her first breath in the capable hands of Dr. Bonnie Merryweather, nobody realized that an honest-to-goodness evil-buster had just arrived in the world. Well, of course, nobody really knew what an evil-buster was, so they weren't prepared to recognize one. No one should be faulted too greatly for not spotting the tell-tale mirror skin and eyes. When Dorina, who was as Waspish as they come, held her first-born in her arms, what she saw was a beautiful, fair-skinned, blue-eyed infant, and it wasn't until some time later—after she read the birth certificate on which Dr. Bonnie, who was African-American, described the child as brown-eyed and of mixed race—that Dorina began to suspect there was something odd about Maxine.

Similarly, when Maxine began to utter her first coherent sounds, it took a while before anyone identified them as echograms. After all, it wasn't really all that unusual for fathers, mothers, grandparents to be convinced that their darling baby's first words were "dada" or "mama" or "nana." But when Maxine was enrolled in the preschool class at Mt. Clarimore Presbyterian Church on Main St., the brilliant Hindu student who was spending the year with the young Bertrand Smith family (and who had agreeably offered to drop Bertrand Smith, Jr., off in the Sunday preschool class) was astonished when Maxine said, just as clearly as President Clinton ever said anything, that "Vishnu is supreme."

"Oh, isn't that sweet," said Sandra Jenkins, who was the senior minister's talented teenage daughter and a Sunday preschool aide. Sandra was helping Maxine take off her coat. "Did you hear that?" Sandra marveled aloud. "Maxine said 'God is love.' Mrs. Brown, I do believe you have a child prodigy here." Dorina Brown heard that last part about the child prodigy unequivocally, but she began to wonder how two smart young students could hear the same words about the Divine One so differently.

Dorina didn't worry about the difference, however, until she left the classroom—and Maxine's presence. The world hadn't yet discovered that that's the way it always works with an evil-buster. Differences are seen, heard, and sometimes noted, but, so long as you are in the presence of an evil-buster, they never seem to matter.

Maybe events would have unfolded in a more desirable fashion had the odds been skewed and had there been one or two more evil-busters born about the same time as Maxine. Maxine was only one individual, and she just simply couldn't be everywhere at once. By the time she was twenty, Maxine was a walking conundrum. She was loved—dearly, authentically, whole-heartedly—wherever she went, for everyone found in her a reflection of what they wanted to find and, being an evil-buster, she somehow had the ability to make these assorted reflections peacefully co-existent. Yet, behind her back, out of the room, they called her a freak, a misfit, and, incredibly, a trouble-maker. Behind her back, out of the room, the discrepancies became apparent and, human nature being what it is, society away from Maxine began to quarrel vociferously. By the time she was twenty-five, the quarreling had turned ugly.

Society's leaders were troubled. The sociologists began to study polarized systems theory. The scientists began to seriously research cloning Maxine, an expensive enterprise about which the politicians were more two-faced than ever. The feminists changed their minds frequently about whether to idolize or denounce Maxine as a representative of the feminine mystique, while the male chauvinists alternately cultivated her attention and popularized derogatory "Maxine" jokes. The economists wanted to market her and the religionists tried to capture her and make her their own.

Maxine began to fear for her safety and sanity. Everyone, it seemed, wanted a piece of her. The poor evil-buster was only a quarter-century old, and already she was tired of being what the mathematicians termed a "chaotic zero-evil attractor." Maxine was only as smart as her beholder—her talent (to bust evil apart) was as an activist, not an intellectual—and so she basically just didn't know what to do about the situation. What Maxine needed was a counterbalance of some sort, an evil-affirmer, so to speak.

As it turned out, Maxine's salvation lay in the grace of God who, being prone (in my opinion) to mathematics, created odds about five times more favorable for the existence of evil-affirmers than for evil-busters, and thereby provided for the absence of boredom, to say nothing of challenge to the human species. With only one in two million billion odds, it really shouldn't be much of a surprise that evil-affirmers—especially those who relish fooling around—would come on the scene at least as quickly as Maxine did, and, indeed, that is how this story was born.

Blackout

T here's a postcard which, until the big blackout of 1997, I've always considered rather clever. It's all black, except, down at the bottom, in white block print, the caption reads "Omaha at night." With one Sunday's unexpected snowstorm, most of the residents of this typical late 20th century Midwestern city began to live in this postcard. A week later many of us were still living there. Somehow the picture didn't seem so clever anymore.

To those of us who limped along on zero power and zero heat, Mother Nature seemed to be sending her own version of the postcard. Only, hers reads: "Omaha in the New Millennium" or, perhaps, "Greetings from Future Society." Or, better yet, "This is your reminder card. You are due for your spirituality check-up."

Overnight, she sent her missive. It arrived so gently that many people slept right through its delivery and woke unsuspecting. The previous day the trees had been laden with leaves that had only barely begun to turn yellow and red. Suddenly they were slathered with heavy snow, which stuck out conspicuously like the white block print on the postcard.

The trees got the message right off. Their limbs cried out at the weight of it, splitting and cracking, so that they soon lay strewn about in total disarray. We humans were slower to grasp the meaning. In fact, I remember looking out my window that first morning and gasping in wondrous awe. Wow! How clever Mother Nature was to send us such an original—and beautiful—card.

One walk along non-existent sidewalks and roads that had disappeared under heavy branches and tangled, broken electric wires soon began to change my mind. The destruction was immense. Omaha resembled a war zone. My joy and delight turned rapidly to concern. The city was deathly quiet. Still, I could hear a faint, unfamiliar, but persistent noise. By the end of the day, I suspected it was the sound of all those gorgeous trees, weeping. After a week of piling blankets on the water bed, sleeping in layers of clothing, lighting candles and trying to heat a three-story house with the burners on our gas stove (in spite of the radio warnings!), I recognized the sound as something else—God's wake-up call.

Now, I figure God talks to us in many ways and this particular message wasn't exactly new. The ecologists, theologists, futurologists have all been relaying their versions of it for some time now, but apparently none of these appeals have been loud enough or strong enough to command our attention. So I reckon God decided to use Mother Nature's voice.

And Mother Nature has a decidedly persuasive way about her. As neighbors helped each other, grew cranky, and then helped each other again, Mother Nature just quietly kept up a constant refrain. As families dealt with no TV, no school, no computers, no phones, no heat, no washing machines, no answering machines, no lamps (no priority intended in this ordering), Mother Nature reminded us: help each other, honor the earth, nurture the trees. As I coped with no e-mail (oh, God, how did I ever survive before the Net?), Mother Nature patiently persuaded us: care for the less fortunate, feed the hungry, shelter the cold, protect the young, enjoy the light, keep the faith.

Scrawled on the back side of that black postcard Nature sent us is a spiritual message no one needs established religion to translate. "Life is about the circulation of the world's generosity. Cherish it and participate."

17

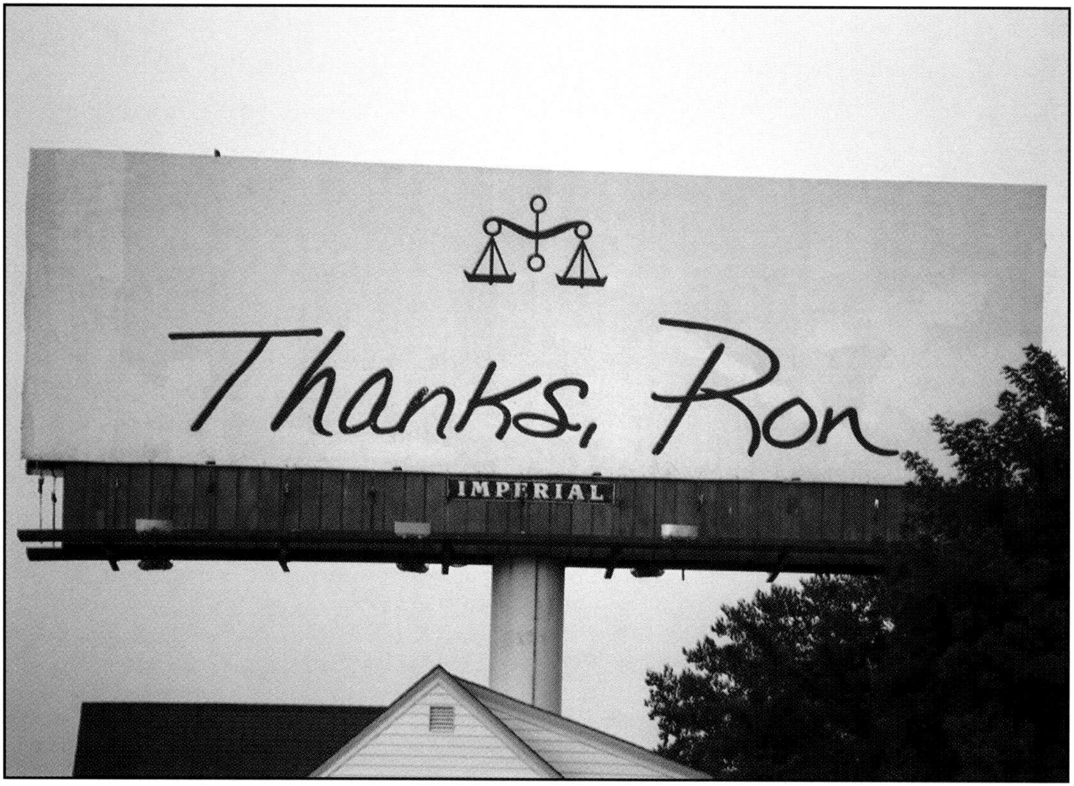
Thanks, Ron
IMPERIAL

Thanks

Where would you start if you wanted to write *A Brief History of Thanks*? You know, answers to the basic questions about gratitude and appreciation: What is thanks? How and when have people given thanks and for what reasons? Why give thanks? Does it come out of nothing, with a sudden burst of energy rather like Hawking's big bang universe? Bugged by such questions, I decided to investigate the tradition of giving thanks and report back in this book.

I went to the library. Into the search computer, I punched $S = subject = thanks$. Guess what came up on the display screen. Lots and lots of listings—all having something to do with *Thanksgiving*. That was just fine if I had wanted to write a brief history of the fourth Thursday in November, but I was looking for something less nation-bound.

I decided to outsmart the machine. I typed in *S* = *thank*, not thanks. Better this time. There were two entries on *thank-you notes* and one on *thankfulness*. And then there were a whole slew of entries on *Thanksgiving*. Dutifully, I jotted down the three possibilities for further research into the history of thanks, and decided to approach the topic from some other direction.

How about checking out *appreciation* instead of *thanks?* I found listings for appreciation of art, appreciation of music, appreciation of painting, and appreciation of sculpture. These were not precisely what I was aiming for, and, furthermore, there were precisely zero entries under each of these headings.

I don't give up easily. I typed in *S* = *gratitude*. There were a few possibilities here. Five possibilities, two of which I had already encountered under *thank*. I jotted down the new ones, then decided to try one last possibility. I typed in *etiquette.*

Bingo! I hit a gold mine. There were addresses, essays, lectures on etiquette. There was etiquette for children and teenagers, etiquette for men, for women. There was Jewish etiquette, Latin American etiquette, business etiquette, diplomatic etiquette, telephone etiquette. There was church etiquette. There was Christian church etiquette. There was the history of etiquette. No doubt, within the fifty-four titles on etiquette, there would be at least some references to thanks—specifically, how to say it properly. I checked out a few of these references. I quickly concluded that, while we may not know how to define thanks, while we may not be able to identify any real sense of what giving thanks is all about or has been all about during the ages, while we may not have paid any real attention to the meaning of giving thanks, or appreciation, or gratitude, we nonetheless are more than willing to tell everybody just exactly how to go about doing it!

Well-armed with my library computer printouts, I delved into everything I could find in the library that in any way related to a history of thanks. Here, briefly, are the four main conclusions I drew.

First, not only is the history of thanks brief, it is almost non-existent. If we want to trace our historical understanding of the nature of thanks, we had better start recording our own present understanding of giving/receiving thanks, appreciation, gratitude one for each other. That way, two thousand years from now, somebody might really be able to trace back a genuine history of thanks.

Second, such history as we do have generally deals with the nature of thanks for the bounty of the harvest. We do, in fact, have a considerable written record of different customs in different countries at different historical periods with regard to the giving of thanks in a manner similar to what we have come to associate with the American November holiday. Check your local newspaper next November if you want to find out more about this particular historical rendering of thanks.

Third, adults seem to be best able to express the nature of thanks by 1) giving gifts (see the etiquette books for proper circumstances and kinds of gifts), 2) writing thank-you notes (see the etiquette books for suggestions on how and when), and 3) singing. Consider Bob Hope's "Thanks for the Memory" or, from the movie version of *A Christmas Carol*, "Thank you very much, thank you very much, that's the nicest thing anyone's ever done for me," or, from *GiGi*, "Thank Heaven for Little Girls." If you are not convinced by this partial listing, let me refer you to most any ordinary church hymnal. "For the beauty of the earth…Source of all, to thee we raise this, our hymn of grateful praise." Or, "Now thank we all our God with heart and hands and voices…." Or, more traditionally, "Give thanks for the corn and the wheat that are reaped, for labor well done and for barns that are heaped…."

Fourth, after searching out the computer's few potential titles dealing with *thanks*, I finally concluded that everything we really need to know about the meaning of thanks we can probably find out best if we look into a child's book. The most explicit expression of what appreciation is all about is in Janet McDonnell's delightful children's book called, simply, *Thankfulness*. Check it out. It's not hard to locate. I found it in the "E" section of the library. That's "E," for "Easiest reading."

Ghosts

Everywhere was the Christmas season—everywhere, that is, except inside my mind. Inside my mind it was the season of dryness. I was six months away from being jobless. I felt betrayed by someone I had trusted. I was too tired to shop for gifts, too depressed to put up a tree, too sorry for myself to write a sermon. Outside my mind people were singing, sleigh bells were ringing. Outside, it was beginning to look like Christmas, but I was beginning to look a lot more like Scrooge than like a minister. Everyone surely had it better than I did. I was back in Omaha and would soon be leaving my husband and daughter for three weeks before the big Ho Ho Ho day. I didn't want to leave them. I did what any self-pitying creature would do. I snapped at Dan and picked a fight with Melinda. Bah. Humbug.

With effort, I forced myself to concentrate on something besides myself. Earlier, I had begun reading a book, *The Eagle's Quest*, which a university professor friend of mine had assigned to one of his classes. Written by Fred Alan Wolf, a physicist who found scientific truth at the heart of the shamanic world, the book had immediately captured my interest, but I had set it aside for a space when I could devote more time to it. Now, I settled into an easy-chair and flipped the book open to a section titled "Time-slips and Sacred Places." I began reading about mysterious occurrences which had taken place near one of the prehistoric stone circles found in Oxfordshire, something about people appearing and disappearing from a road which was built atop radioactive rock.

"Paul believes that the experiences were essentially time-slips," I read. "The car was going to come, or had been there the day before, or week before or whatever. The same is true for the gypsy caravan."

I yawned. I realized I was going to have to get more exercise. Maybe that would give me more energy.

I read on. "...It was an old route where caravans could have gone in that particular area..."

I found myself intrigued by the notion that within the mind there might be some sort of shift which could allow time-slips to occur. I began to skim the narration a little, trying to get a sense of where the author was headed. Intermittently, I found the narration getting mixed up with my personal worries. Six months. Jobless. Boy, it was hard to stay focused on the book—on *any* book. Boy, I was tired.

Suddenly, I looked up, realizing I was no longer alone in the room. A man dressed for bed, complete with nightshirt and nightcap, stood by the door. He looked like something out of a Dickens novel.

"Oh!" I said and jumped visibly in my seat.

"Who are you?" he asked in a deep, authoritative voice.

"Who am I," I asked, somewhat indignantly. "Who are *you*? And what are you doing in my house?"

"*Your* house?" He looked around thoughtfully for a moment. "Oh, my goodness, I must have done another time-slip." He seemed a little nonplused. "You aren't another one of those ghosts, are you? I don't think I could take anymore of those encounters just now!"

"What do you mean, am I a ghost?" I said. I was really surprised. Some people get ministers mixed up with everything. "No, I'm not a ghost. I'm a minister."

Now he was the one who looked really surprised. "Come on, you're a woman." With a wave of his hand, he dismissed the idea as preposterous. Then he looked me over more thoughtfully, as though the fact of my womaness were fully registering. "What are you," he asked, frowning slightly, but not with any malice, "the Ghost of My Fantasy World?"

I straightened my posture from my slumped position in the easy chair and ironed a couple of imaginary wrinkles from my blue jeans and shirt. Suddenly I wished I were dressed more professionally. "I'm the Rev. Dr. Sarah Voss," I said standing tall with as much command as I could muster. "Now, who are you?"

"The Rev. Dr., eh!" He started to smile, took off his nightcap and made an exaggerated bow. "Well, now I've heard everything. Bah! Humbug!" But he said it nicely. I found myself relaxing.

Then it hit me. "You're Scrooge, aren't you?" I asked.

"How'd you know that?" He appeared genuinely shocked.

"I'm a Unitarian Universalist minister," I replied quickly. "Unitarian Universalists know such things."

"What else do you know?" I sensed he was testing me.

"Oh, not much. Just that you were visited by the Ghost of Christmas Past, the Ghost of Christmas Present, and the Ghost of Christmas Future and before they visited you were a mean, depressed, bitter old man who didn't care a hoot about anything but money, but after they visited, you cleaned up your act so that you wouldn't die a lonely, hated old miser."

"Dear God," he said, and somehow I don't think he was saying it in vain. "What kind of a minister did you say you were?"

"Oh, I know a lot about you, all right," I said, then added, more to myself than to him, "but I don't know why you are here. Why are you here, anyway?"

He crumpled his cap into a tight wad, smoothed it out, then crumpled it again. "I don't think I know why I'm here," he replied. "Unless you are—well, unless you really are the Ghost of My Fantasy or some such thing. That's been my only experience with time-slips."

"Sorry," I said, "but I'm just a Unitarian Universalist with a particularly active imagination."

He began then to really look around my home. He took in the computer, the modem, the mini-blinds at the windows. "That must have been some time-slip," he said. "Where are we in time, anyway?"

"It's late 20th century. At least I think it is." I looked out the window. Same Nebraska houses across the street. Same big old maples with their slight covering of frost. "Yes, November," I added, with some assurance.

"Wow! You're the hyper-future," he whispered, awed. "Tell me, what's your world like?"

"Oh, you know. There's a lot of drug abuse, lots of violence. Hunger. Poverty. Wars all over. Peace treaties made in the Middle East, but not honored. Kids shooting kids just to prove that they can belong to a gang in the United States. Policemen selling ten-year-olds for money in Brazil. World-wide joblessness. Lots of soullessness. Lots of racial, gender, age prejudice. Half of all marriages end in divorce. One fourth of all children in Iowa are born out of wedlock. The world has 6.5 billion people and a growth rate that won't stop. Many people expect to see a nuclear war within their lifetime. Christmas is nothing but a buy and sell market. Nobody seems to care about anyone anymore."

He studied me carefully. "Did you have a bad day?" he finally ventured.

Even I had to smile. "Well, I guess I *am* a bit down-hearted and negative."

"Humph!"

"But, Scrooge," I said with sudden seriousness, "our world really does seem pretty sorry these days. It's like, well, it's as though things are out of control. Why, I read the other day that murder now ranks as the third most frequent cause of death in America's work-place. My friend in Cedar Rapids, whose mother lives in England, says its not any better in your country either. And, not long ago, I heard someone admit that they have begun to be afraid even in a nice little town like Cedar Rapids, Iowa. What's happening, Scrooge? Why can't people seem to learn the lessons your ghosts taught you—taught us? Why can't people treat their environment kindly and live in peace with each other?

Scrooge shook his head sadly. "I thought things *would* get better. They got better for me when I started giving," he said. "In fact, the more I gave, the better things got."

"Well, yes, of course," I replied, a little briskly. "Everybody *knows* that. But we don't *do* it, except once a year at Christmas-time. Maybe."

"Ummm."

For a few moments, neither of us said anything at all. I stared absently at the photographs I keep tacked all over the wall behind my computer. There were the kids when they were little, Dan at our marriage a year ago, a picture of Peoples Church taken when I came to interview for the position of interim minister. Oh, and there was that picture of me as a little girl with my grandparents. Grandpa, pipe in mouth, was sitting on one side of the kitchen table, his cards all laid out for his nightly game of solitaire. Grandma sat on the other side, sewing.

"Look, Scrooge," I said, pointing to the picture. "That's my grandmother and grandfather. I'm sure life wasn't always perfect for them, but somehow they always seemed to keep hope about them. Boy, I wish I could talk with them now."

"Why don't we try?"

"What?"

"Try. A time-slip." He held out his hand.

When I reached for him, I actually expected something magical might happen. Something did, only it was not what I expected. No grandparents materialized. No conversation with them ensued.

Instead, when Scrooge and I joined hands, for one wonderful, incredible moment, the entire wall opened up like a 3-D movie screen you could walk into. Suddenly, in the spot where we'd been looking at photographs, there was an old, open manger. People mulled about it, as though it were a live nativity scene. This was real!

Well, no, of course it wasn't real. Yet it seemed real. I even heard the slight, distinctive sound of a newborn baby's cry. The baby Jesus, I thought instantly. It was a cry, yet I could make out the meaning, almost as though actual words were being sounded. "This is a picture of hope," the baby cried, or said. "Take it and translate it into something appropriate for your time."

"Wow," I gasped. "Scrooge, did you hear what I heard?"

No sooner had I spoken aloud than the scene disappeared, and Grandma and Grandpa were back in their 3"X5" space on the wall. "Scrooge," I said turning to him, but he, too, was gone.

At once, I heard a loud bump. I looked down and saw that the book I had been reading had fallen to the floor. Maybe I've been asleep, I thought. Maybe I've been dreaming.

I bent to retrieve the book. Yes, that surely was it. I'd been dreaming. Time-slips only happen in books or dreams.

But as I picked up the book, I noticed a card stuck in it that I didn't remember seeing before. Curious, I examined it, noting that it was a Christmas card, one depicting the nativity scene, Star of Bethlehem and all.

"I wonder where that came from?" I said, half-aloud. I opened it, noting that it was unsigned. In fact, it was one of those blank greeting cards, except someone had written on it. "Picture of hope," I read scrawled across the space. The handwriting looked suspiciously like my own. "Place in your heart."

I smiled to myself. Maybe it had all been a dream. Maybe it had been a warning. Maybe it had been a gift.

Compassion

My father taught me three important lessons about the meaning of "compassion." In the first lesson, he used the word directly and I was left to fill in the meaning from the situation. In retrospect, this is no huge surprise, for I was very young and that was how I learned the meaning of most words.

My father had killed a cow. I'm not sure that anyone actually told me he had killed her, but somehow I knew. I was curious: What did a killed cow look like? But it quickly became apparent that I was not going to get to see the cow. What I saw was my father, his face drawn and tight, carrying his shotgun into the farmhouse and locking it up again in the oak gun cabinet that stood in the little hallway by the bathroom.

As a six- or seven-year-old, I had already discovered that nobody talked directly to you about such things and that it was far more productive just to keep your eyes wide and your ears open. Like most children of mid-twentieth century America—and probably like most children everywhere—I was good at watching and listening. The cow, I discovered, had been "pregnant," which I already knew meant she was going to have a calf. I also knew that, left alone, cows about to give birth normally choose to wander away from the rest of the herd, finding some secluded, private spot where they can bring their calf into the world without interruption.

The cow my father killed had been just such a cow. Usually, my father would watch for the signs of impending birth and, when the time seemed near, would segregate the animal in the barn where she could be "helped," should she need such help. This cow had fooled him, sneaking off alone, not returning to the barn with the rest of the herd for the evening milking and meal. It wasn't until early the next morning that she was found and by then it was too late. She had made herself a little nest in the brush by the back pond. After hours of "labor," another word defined only by the resulting calf, she had gotten into "trouble." If she'd been inside the barn, she could have been helped, but, as it was, off there in the wilderness by herself, something went too wrong to be fixed. My father shot the cow to put her out of her misery. It was—and here I heard the word for the first time—the "compassionate" thing to do.

Lesson number one: compassion has something to do with misery, with suffering, or, more specifically, with putting an end to suffering.

Lesson number two happened some half dozen years later, but still on the farm. My father was raking and my older brother and I were baling hay one hot summer day. Haying was, minimally, a two-man, i.e., two-person, job. Someone mowed the hay and, later, raked it into neat rows. Someone else then drove alongside on a tractor, pulling a baler and wagon. The baler gobbled up the soft mounds of hay, formed them into neat rectangles tied with twine, and spat them out onto the wagon, where someone strong stacked them five bales wide and seven or eight bales high. On this particular day we were a three-man job: my father raked the field ahead of us and I drove the tractor which pulled the baler and wagon while my brother heaved the bales into their high stacks. At twelve, I was still a little girl, but puffed up with pride at being able to handle a "man's" job, a job which, incidentally, I'd been doing since I was ten. Dennis had a different perspective. At eighteen, soon to head off to college, he was stuck for hours with his younger sister on a dirty, dusty, sweaty, tiring job which was disgustingly boring. He couldn't find anything good to say about anyone just then.

My brother's sour mood wasn't much of a problem as long as it was me he could abuse with his sullenness. However, when the three of us stopped late in the afternoon for a ginger-water break, he began venting his displeasure freely. Most of it, predictably, was leveled at me. I couldn't drive well, didn't watch out for the rocks which plugged up the baler (a lie, even to this day, an unfair lie!), was a creep, an idiot, and so on. I don't remember the exact words, only the emotion. My brother was sullen, and, somehow, it was all my fault. I hung my head in shame.

My father rarely interfered in the relationship between my brother and me, preferring to leave it to the two of us to work out. However, he also didn't normally see this side of my brother, and, to be honest, I didn't always see it either. It wasn't always there. On this occasion, however, my brother was nastier than ever, prompting our father to intervene. He drew my brother off to the side, but not so far away that I couldn't hear. Placing his hand firmly on Dennis's arm, he quietly told him that I was the only little sister he would ever have, that I didn't deserve that kind of treatment, and that he ought not to do that any more. My father never even raised his voice, yet my brother was subdued. After that, he was more careful about how he talked to me. It was such a rare occurrence to be supported in this fashion that now, forty years later, I can still recall how good it felt.

Lesson number two: compassion helps reduce the suffering. Compassion feels good. It heals.

Lesson number three also occurred on the farm. I was a newly married twenty-two year-old college student. It was Christmas-time and we three siblings had gathered in the old farmhouse with our spouses and kids to celebrate the occasion.

Things were changing rapidly for our family. My father had been ill for several years and had reluctantly sold the farm. He and Mother would be moving in the spring into a "city" home. Because we knew this would be our last time together in the home where we had all grown up, my brother and sister and I had all juggled our schedules so that we could be together for at least part of the holiday.

A week before that Christmas, Dad had another heart attack, a fairly serious one, we were told. We went home fully expecting to have to visit him in the hospital, but, to our pleasant surprise, he was waiting for us at home. We were so happy to have him home that it didn't matter that he was recuperating in the bedroom. We laughed and joked, carried our meals into the bedroom rather than to the dining room.

We celebrated Christmas on Christmas Eve because we were leaving early the next morning. What a wonderful Christmas Eve that was! Dad was too tired to go to the livingroom where the tree was, so we gathered around his bed to open presents. I can't remember a single one of the gifts we exchanged that year…but, of course, the real gift was our being all together. Dad said it was his best Christmas yet. He grew a little teary, then, but over the past few years we had gradually learned to accept his emotionalism as part of his recovery process. The next morning we kissed him goodbye and told him we loved him, and that he should rest a lot so that he could get well soon. He nodded, smiling, and told us, once again, how glad he was that we had all come.

Dad always said he'd rather wear out than rust out, but none of us expected him to wear out so soon. Dad was fifty-nine when he died that Christmas day. The highway patrol caught up with us a few hundred miles down the road, and we all turned around and went back home. What had happened, we wanted to know? He had seemed to be doing so well! Only later did we learn that his doctor had found a large clot in his heart which was not responding to medicine. Dad had begged him to let him go home to die. He never once let on that he knew his time was up. He hung on just long enough for us to have a truly joyous time together.

Compassion lesson number three: compassion means "to suffer with." Quite literally, the word is derived from two Latin roots, one of which means "to suffer" and the other, "with." I used to think that "to suffer with" meant you had to feel bad, to be actively suffering along with the other person. If you weren't suffering, how could you be really compassionate? Well, true enough, we were all suffering on Christmas day, and we were "with" each other—but that wasn't what this final lesson of my father's was all about. It's taken me years to grasp what my father's final gift to us all was. "To suffer with," compassionately, means "to *be* with during the suffering." My father's sorrows were great. And, although we didn't fully appreciate just how greatly he was suffering, we were with him in his sorrow. We were fully, totally, happily with him. My father didn't want us to be suffering, too. He just wanted company on his own sad trip. I think, now, that if he could have, he would have shared his sorrow with us more openly. But he couldn't trust us to know enough about compassion to resist the temptation to wallow in our own sorrow. Instead, he *showed* us what real compassion means, by arranging his last moments with us in such a way that we experienced the fullness of our joy in being with him, even in his grief.

When I was born, I knew nothing about compassion. I was a blank slate— a big zero, at least in the realm of compassion. I was one of the lucky ones. I had a father who knew how to color in that zero so that it turned into a full sun.

Words

J eff and Jerry were identical twins, identical in every outward appearance except for one. For some unexplained reason Jeff was born mute. Not deaf and mute, just mute.

When the twins were little, it had been kind of cute. Jerry was an early talker, and Jeff would mimic whatever he said—without words, of course. As he grew older, however, Jeff found his muteness more of a handicap than cute. Anyone who has ever had a severe case of laryngitis will probably appreciate some of Jeff's frustrations. When they discovered that Jeff couldn't say any words, folks would usually either break into a whisper and start writing him notes, or yell loudly, as though overcompensating for his muteness might somehow eliminate the problem. Being the identical twin of a loquacious talker, Jeff experienced an additional complication. People who didn't know he was a twin would engage in some fantastic conversation with Jerry and, then, seeing Jeff and mistaking him for Jerry, they would take "refusal" to talk as rudeness, obstinacy, or even anti-social behavior.

As a consequence, Jeff, being every bit as bright as Jerry, sought out ways to counteract the negative reactions his muteness tended to elicit. He became a mime. All the world loves a mime, and Jeff was as good as they come. When he was seven, he began painting his face white and he took mime lessons. When he was fifteen, he began wearing his white face every hour of the day, regardless of whether or not he was "performing." He wore it to school, to church, to the Wellingtons' wedding and to old Mrs. Barton's funeral. Those who knew him best began to be concerned. Some even thought his attitude was indicative of more anti-social behavior, but most of them were generally pretty tolerant people and they more or less figured it was just a stage he would eventually outgrow.

The stage lasted three years. When they were eighteen, the twins went to separate colleges and, one month after he was settled into his new dorm, Jeff decided that the white face would have to go. He was enrolled in Psychology 101 and he began to suspect that he was "hiding" behind the white face. Consequently, he took it off.

For the next four years, he refused to wear it at all and declined to give any more mime performances. That was a shame because he was so good at them, but it may have helped him pay attention to his studies. Yet, without the comfort and safety of the mask he'd worn for so long, he truly did become somewhat reclusive. He spent long hours at the library or sitting at his desk behind the computer, where words could be written rather than said and he could put them together like any other person. In fact, he developed quite a facility as a writer, for, in spite of his not being able to utter any words, he became a master at crafting them together. When he was graduated from college, he was already making a name for himself as a freelance writer, a career he decided to pursue.

Ten books (three of them best sellers), numerous articles, one wife and two children later, Jeff began to suspect that he was hiding behind his writing every bit as much as he had hidden behind his white face. Who was he, with or without words? With words, he was a highly-regarded, albeit silent, author and the winner of several prestigious literary awards. Was this who he was? Was this his true identity? What if he hadn't become a successful author, but, rather, was just a mediocre writer who never quite made it? Would he be someone different then, or was there a Jeff underneath the writing veneer that was not being revealed? Without words, he was an entertainer, albeit a silent one. As an entertainer, he engaged others and connected with them in ways which were both humorous and rewarding. Was this his true identity? Where was the Jeff who existed without regard to words? Plagued by such questions, Jeff had a classic mid-life crisis.

While he was in the grip of this crisis, Jeff was a basket case. His marriage became shaky. His writing floundered. He grew irritable and depressed. He hired out for children's birthday parties and other events as a sad clown, and began to think of himself in that fashion. Life didn't have a whole lot of laughs in it, even though he was still able to bring laughter into the lives of others. Oddly, he began to realize that he felt best about himself when he was wearing his white clown's face. He decided he needed a major change in his life. He gave up writing and opened a clown school.

There was a great deal to learn about being in a small education business for oneself, and soon Jeff was totally engrossed in the clown school. It was as though he'd received a shot in the arm. Suddenly he had energy again. Suddenly he was busy and productive and, yes, even happy. His mid-life crisis vanished. It wasn't that he had discovered the answers to all those questions about identity which had plagued him earlier. He was just too busy to care.

Jeff spent the next two decades making his clown school prosper. It grew in reputation so that prospective clowns from all over the states, and even some from abroad, sought out the school. Jeff's youngest child, a girl, went through the program and then discovered a natural inclination for the business end of the operation. When he turned sixty-two, Jeff sold the business to his daughter and he and his wife, who had somehow managed to weather all the crises of their wedded life, decided to travel.

They sold their home, purchased a late-model mobile van with all the toys and accessories, and spent the next four years as itinerant campers. Wherever they camped, Jeff would offer impromptu mime shows, which earned him a modest reputation as a traveling mime. He was gray-haired now, and his face was naturally kind of pale and white, although he still used the white-face when he was performing. One summer the *New York Times* even did a life-style article about "Grandpa Mime," as he was affectionately known, and *Modern Maturity* picked up on the article, turning it into an inspirational piece for senior citizens.

As he grew even older, Jeff developed a new interest in spiritual matters. Faith issues became a matter of intense interest to him. He and his wife moved into a condominium near their older child—the one who had settled down into traditional family life. When Jeff learned that one of his grandsons had apparently inherited his own muteness, he made it a point to spend extra time with the child. He took the child for long walks in a nearby forest and he taught him everything he could about the art of silent communication. It became important to Jeff that he pass something of his life on. At an elder hostel, Jeff signed up for a course in memoir writing, and he began to write his life story. Then he and his grandson turned it into live theater—silent, of course. The grandpa/grandson pair performed the drama at a neighborhood art institute, where it received raves of applause. A local reviewer wrote that it was "a heart-warming interpretation of faith at work."

Jeff outlived his wife by about two years and his brother Jerry by two months. On his deathbed he was a contented man, for he realized that he had enjoyed a full and rich life. It was curious, he thought, that he had done so without even once uttering a single word.

Profanity

As a child, my youngest was an adorable, petite girl who, with her long blond curls, always looked somewhat angelic. One snowy day when she was five, she and the five-year old girl next door were sledding down the hill in front of our house, on my daughter's brand new, bright red saucer sled. Bill, the "older" boy from across the street apparently decided he'd like to try out that new sled for himself. He intended to do so, with or without their permission. Without, as it turned out. The girls were not in the sharing mood.

Bill, who was about fourteen, was bigger and stronger, so he did what the bigger and stronger have done for eons—he took the sled. What he had not counted on was my darling little angel's vocabulary. With unqualified expertise, she put her hands on her hips and, at the top of her lungs, spat out a

stream of verbal venom that would have challenged the most proficient macho adult curser. Certainly it challenged Bill. He was so stunned that he dropped the sled and left. It wasn't that he was afraid, mind you: you'll remember that he was considerably bigger and stronger than these two little girls. Somehow, knowing the teenagers in that neighborhood, I doubt that he was unfamiliar with the general nature of this profanity either. Apparently he was just so astonished to be hearing it streaming out of the mouth of such a sweet-appearing female package that he was totally confused.

I was confused, too, when Rick, the other little girl's father, told me a couple of days later how he had overheard this incident. From what he said, I wondered how anyone could have helped overhearing. Then I wondered where I had been, because I hadn't heard a thing. I gleaned from Rick's manner that he had wondered about that as well, but he didn't actually say anything. Then I wondered if he had wondered about just exactly where my sweet little five-year-old angel had heard such language. I blushed at the thought, but quickly got control of myself. This line of wondering was not one I cared to pursue too closely. After all, ours was a family establishment.

I knew what it meant to be a family establishment in middle-class America. It meant that if you're the mother of a five-year-old girl caught in the act of loud profanity, you are supposed to address the matter with your child. To this day, I can't remember how, or even if I had a heart-to-heart with my youngest and most innocent about the impropriety of her verbal outburst. What I remember is the discomfort of being caught in my own double standard.

My daughter, you see, just hadn't picked up on my full lesson, which went something like this: It's okay to swear, but don't swear in front of grandmothers or others who would find the swearing offensive. And never, ever, stand with your hands on your hips in the front yard yelling your head off with loud profanity. Then everyone will *know*.

"That everyone will *know*" is the first sin I learned about in the tiny town where I grew up. "Don't hang your dirty linen out to dry, or everyone will know." It was such an important sin that I didn't understand why it wasn't listed in the Bible. People in our small town knew about the Bible, and they knew whether or not your family studied it every Sunday at the local church. This was another inexplicable application of this first great sin. Not only did everyone *know* if you were not among those who made this weekly pilgrimage, but if you actually were among those good folk attending church, then it was okay for everyone to know this fact about your family. More than that—it was *important* that everyone know.

It took me years before I was able to *name* this double standard about the great sin of letting everybody know, but it didn't take me any time at all to catch on to the fact of it. Why, when I was five years old, I'd rather have died than be caught letting everyone *know* about things they weren't supposed to know about. Punishment for such sin was swift and severe.

Now, this incident taught me about one other great sin that isn't listed in the Bible, but of course I had to grow up before I could recognize it. It goes something like this: if your child is caught in the act of sinning, then it's your fault and your responsibility. Wow! To commit that sin, I have discovered over the years, is to commit an act so loaded with the profane that redemption is virtually impossible. Jewish mothers may have more insight into this than other mothers, or fathers for that matter, but that's only hearsay and may just be an old wive's tale. The fact of the matter is that the sins of the child are visited upon the parents, most likely the mother. God may forgive such sins, but the establishment is usually not so generous.

You think I'm exaggerating? Well, may you have kids of your own, and then you'll know.

Games

In the beginning there were no games at all; there was only boredom and quiet. Then God created zero-sum games. These are games like chess, poker, bridge, and tic tac toe, where two players (or teams) follow specified rules and one player wins and one player loses, so that the end result is both constant and zero. War can be thought of as a zero-sum game, though often it requires more than two players. God labeled such games high-level competition games. That is, winner takes all.

God watched in fascination as the various creatures in the world he had created engaged in zero-sum games. The most interesting were the last ones he'd created, the humans. For God had stacked the deck, so-to-speak, by hard-wiring in these humans the desire to have dominion over all the other creatures. The humans not only constantly played zero-sum games, but they

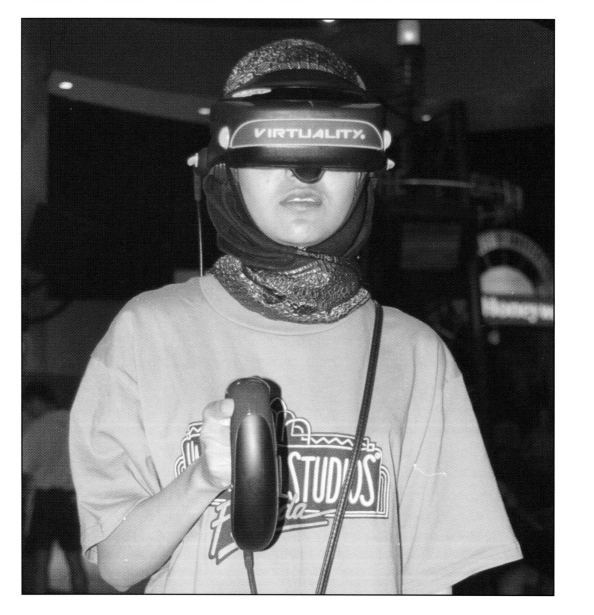

also had that extra natural incentive to make sure they were the winners. Strictly speaking, this factor kept them from playing games of perfect information, since it could be argued that not all the creatures playing the game had access to all the information. In particular, not all the creatures knew that humans assumed the right of victory.

For a long time, God rested and relaxed, just watching how these zero-sum games played out but making no move to interfere in the outcomes. After thousands of years, God was shocked to see that the humans were not just winning; in the process of winning they were annihilating everything else he had created. Thus, in order to introduce the humans to alternative strategies and outcomes, God created virtual reality. Humans took to virtual reality just as they had to zero-sum games—they tried to "win." So God let them.

On the first day of virtual play the humans set off a massive nuclear detonation which wiped out all the children, the smallest, newest, and most dependent creatures in the world. On the second day of virtual play the beasts of the earth, cattle of all kinds, and all things that creep on the earth were obliterated. On the third day of virtual play nuclear pollution spread to the waters and the skies, and all the sea creatures and every bird of the air died. On the fourth day of virtual play, pollution clouded earth's atmosphere so that the sun and stars disappeared from sight and it became impossible to distinguish day from night. On the fifth day light disappeared altogether and everything was left in darkness. On the sixth day of virtual play the nuclear cloud interfered with the heavenly gravitational pull, and the earth shattered into particles of such small dimension that they were for all practical purposes nonexistent.

The humans who were playing this virtual reality game grew concerned. "Oh, dear God," they exclaimed, "this situation is not good. Can you possibly help us?"

And God looked with pity upon these creatures whom he had favored, for he realized they had not understood that, by invoking free will, a constant-sum game doesn't always have to be zero. They were poor imitations of real mathematicians, these humans, although God was still rather fond of them. Being of a basically benevolent and forgiving nature, God decided to treat them with mercy. Besides, he was growing rather tired of purely competitive strategies. So God created a new category of game.

These new games were still games of strategy, but now they also included an element of bargaining. Not wishing to eliminate free will, God designed them so they could be either cooperative or non-cooperative depending, for example, on whether or not there is communication between the players. Peace was one such game, although it was one which depended upon cooperation. God called these new games non-zero-sum games, and he looked at them and saw that they were good. And then God rested again.

Olive

It had been a long, particularly trying day at the church, the kind of day when it seemed as though everyone I talked to was harboring some sort of resentment towards someone else and putting someone else down. It gets pretty exhausting after a while. Anyway, I had rushed to the mall on my way home and quickly purchased a couple of gifts. When I finally opened my front door, I stashed the packages in the hallway closet, yelled "I'm home" to Melinda upstairs, and flipped on the TV, hoping to catch some late news. Then I collapsed on the couch. I would sit down for just a few minutes before I fixed supper. I tried not to think of all the things I needed to get done in the next few days before Christmas.

Then the oddest thing happened. One moment they were talking about the troubled European situation, and the news commentator started to cut

in with a map of Yugoslavia, only it turned out not to be Yugoslavia at all, but the North Pole. The next thing I knew, two figures were walking through the snow toward some sort of barn-like structure. As the TV cameras zoomed in, I realized with a start that the two figures were Jesus and Mrs. Claus, and that they were deeply engaged in conversation. This is weird, I thought. I wasn't so sure I liked the idea of television capturing Mrs. Claus and Jesus together like that. Somehow it seemed, well, sort of improper. As a minister, I'm particularly sensitive to the secular turn which our society seems to have taken. When Santa Claus was first invented in 1822 by New York professor of theology Clement C. Moore in his now-famous ballad, "The Night Before Christmas," it was the first step toward making Christmas "Xmas." Forty years later, during the American Civil War, cartoonist Thomas Nast sketched for *Harper's* magazine the jovial, plump, costumed character depicted in Moore's story. Just who decided Santa Claus needed to have a Mrs., I haven't been able to discover, but she too was invented, to make him socially acceptable. Now Santa Claus is more real for many people than is the man born roughly two thousand years ago in a manger in the little city of Bethlehem.

Speaking of whom…there he was, strolling alongside Mrs. Claus right on my livingroom television screen. I know TV distorts reality somewhat, but I must say I was surprised. Jesus was clad in white robes as you might expect, but he was dark-skinned. He looked pretty Mid-Eastern to me, which, I suppose shouldn't have been a surprise seeing as how he was born in Bethlehem.

I thought he had a Jewish look about him, too. And he looked older than my image of him. But I told myself it *has* been almost two thousand years, even if you allow for the bad record keeping which must have occurred somewhere along the line. Jesus was born, according to the gospel of St. Matthew, when Herod was still alive and, according to some authorities, Herod died around the year 4 B.C., which means Jesus must have been born around 6 B.C., which makes him six years older than we normally think of him.

Anyway, Jesus and Mrs. Claus were on the TV local news, and, as a minister, I wasn't sure I liked it. Of course, as a minister, I think it's important that I keep an open mind. Why, if it weren't for open minds, I never would have become a minister in the first place, my being a woman and all. It wasn't so very long ago that folks generally considered a woman being a minister more or less like making a fiction out of something sacred, like turning something holy into a joke.

When I thought of it this way, it suddenly didn't seem so outrageous that Jesus and Mrs. Claus were walking and talking together on my television screen. You could tell that they were deeply engaged in conversation, but you couldn't make out any words—must have been a technical foul-up of some sort at the television station. That happens a lot. We've got all this marvelous technology—satellite viewing, instant replays, simulated worlds so real you get mixed up as to what is real and what isn't. Basically I like it. It's changed the way we look at the world. Why, today we have pictures of the Earth from far, far away, so that it looks like a tiny blue ball, a Christmas ornament, so to speak, hanging from God's sky. But some glitch is always happening in the hardware, so that you can never be sure you're getting the whole view of things. Like now, when Jesus and Mrs. Claus were talking—somehow the sound wasn't coming through. I was irritated because it looked as though what they were saying was important.

No sooner had I become aware of my irritation than the strangest—and I do mean the strangest—thing happened to me that I have ever experienced. This warm light shot out of the TV screen and all at once I was surrounded by light. I don't know how to explain this, but it somehow lifted me off the couch and carried me, yes, carried me, toward the TV set—and not only toward it, but *into* it. I remember thinking, oh, no, they warned us that watching too much TV would warp your mind! Then, the next thing I knew, I was *there*. I mean, I was right there at the North Pole with Jesus and Mrs. Claus, and I could hear every word they were saying.

Evidently Santa had been catching a nap so he would be well-rested for his travels and Mrs. Claus was on her way to tend to the reindeer when Jesus had suddenly materialized along her path. She appeared nonplused by this miraculous appearance. I gathered from the general tone of their conversation that they knew each other rather well. They were talking about Yugoslavia and lamenting how the human species always seemed to be turning simple religious differences into bloody battles and Jesus was saying something about how nothing he had ever preached should have led to warfare. In fact it was totally contrary to his basic message of peace and love. He seemed kind of discouraged. Mrs. Claus listened and nodded sympathetically. To my mind, she was actually a little too sympathetic and nurturing. In this day and age when men and women are constantly struggling with equal rights issues and the empowerment of minorities, I can't help wondering if Mrs. Claus doesn't need to change her image a bit.

On the other hand, Jesus *was* pretty sad. After two thousand years of pushing love and hope, it has to be pretty disheartening to see some of the stuff that is still going on. Why, in our age of plenty, there are still humans starving to death—and the best solution people have come up with so far seems to be a show of guns and force as some sort of mercy mission. That's a far cry from the "Golden Rule" Jesus championed. So far as I could tell from what he was saying, Jesus championed the rule, not the religious wrapping in which it was dressed. "Do unto others as you would have them do unto you." It doesn't matter whether you say it as a Jew, a Christian, a Muslim, a Buddhist, a Hindu—whether you say it in Hebrew, English, Greek, or Somalian. What matters is that you say it, and mean it, and live it. At least that's what I understood Jesus to be saying, as he and Mrs. Claus walked toward the reindeer.

I followed along, about ten paces behind them, but in plain sight so they wouldn't think I was intruding. I know they saw me, but they didn't pay me any attention, so I figured they didn't mind my listening in. They were pretty engrossed in their talk. Then, as they neared the stalls by the barn, Rudolph bounded up. He was a magnificent looking creature—and his red lamp of a nose was everything I had ever imagined it to be. It glowed, like a star, and lit up the snowy surroundings. I could see why Santa wanted him to guide the sleigh. In a way, Rudolph's red nose was a kind of technology for the North Pole.

"Wow, Rudolph," Mrs. Claus was saying. "No wonder Olive was jealous. Poor, poor Olive. You know, Jesus, poor Olive is the one I'm really concerned about. We ought to go feed Olive."

"Olive?" I wondered. I went through the list. Dancer. Prancer. Donner. Blitzen. Maybe they knew something I didn't. "Who's Olive?" I asked. I hadn't realized I had spoken aloud until that moment when Jesus and Mrs. Claus both turned to me. "Oh, hi, Sarah," they said, and it seemed like the most natural thing in the world to be standing there at the North Pole with Mrs. Claus and Jesus. "Olive is the other reindeer," Mrs. Claus explained patiently. "You know, the one who laughed and called Rudolph names."

"And wouldn't let him join in any of the games." Jesus added.

"Oh," I said. I couldn't think of anything more intelligent to say. "Oh," I repeated. Then I burst out in roaring, somewhat jeering laughter. "Why, that's absurd," I said. "That's stupid. Everyone knows that it's not Olive that laughed and called him names. It's *all of. All of* the other reindeer used to laugh and call him names." I wagged my finger at them. "Olive. That's the most ridiculous thing I've ever heard. Don't you two know anything?"

I doubled over in laughter, holding my stomach, I thought it was so funny, and suddenly they were fading. "Wait," I said. "Wait, don't go. I didn't mean anything."

But it was too late. Suddenly, I was back on my couch and there was a commercial showing on the television set. I sat there, for a long time, staring blankly at the TV screen, pondering what I had just experienced. I thought about all the people in the world who laughed and jeered at someone else because they were or thought or acted "different." I thought of the people in Somalia. I thought of the people in Yugoslavia. I thought of the people I had run into that very day, the ones who always seemed to be judging and putting someone else down. And then I thought about me, and about how quick I had been to wag my finger at Mrs. Claus and Jesus.

I felt pretty sick inside. Here I had had this wonderful opportunity to be with Jesus and Mrs. Claus, and I had messed it up. Worse, I had been judgmental and mocking. Me. A minister. The longer I thought, the worse I felt.

Suddenly there were footsteps overhead, and Melinda came bounding downstairs. She carried a big box in her hands. "Mom," she said, "this was outside the door when I came home from school."

Together we opened it. It was filled with cookies and fruit and cheeses and crackers. It was beautiful. Somebody clearly cared. I felt better already.

"Oh, I almost forgot," Melinda added, "a really weird note came with it." She dashed upstairs again and, returning a minute later, she handed me a plain white card. On it, penned it an old-fashioned script, was a simple message. "Food for Olive. With love, Santa."

"Who's Olive, Mom?" she asked.

Slowly, a warm, wonderful feeling arose within me and the world, this world, seemed to me like an amazingly perfect place to be just then. I put my arm around my daughter's shoulder and together we started toward the kitchen. "Well, Melinda," I said, "let me tell you about Olive. Olive, the other reindeer."

Stones

Not long ago I had the thrill of exploring some old stone circles in Ireland: mathematical conundrums of ancient times. Unlike Stonehenge, these were touchable stones. However, they were very difficult to touch in that they were hard to locate and involved tramping through a great deal of very wet bog—the kind that leaves inappropriate footwear soaked and more or less permanently smelly.

It was clear from the assorted objects left on two flat rocks within this circle of ancient stones that others had made the journey as well.

I was fascinated and overcome by the awe of the old, mixed with the timeless beauty of nature. A part of me suspected that there were fairies in the wild bushes watching, waiting. I'm not a pagan. I had no rituals adequate to the task of being there in this obviously "sacred" spot. I was left with a strong personal need to improvise something "appropriate" for this pilgrimage.

I examined the objects on the rock altars more closely. I even picked up one of the braided crowns of grass and stuck it on my head, posing for my spouse to take a snapshot, which he obligingly did. I wanted to take this crown home with me as a remembrance of the occasion, but somehow it didn't feel like the right thing to do, so, reluctantly, I put it back. I looked for something else to sequester away in my suitcase: a stone, a shell, a twig—anything at all from this mathematical place of worship. My desire to have became a ripe yearning. Whatever the secrets of this place, I wanted them. And, if I couldn't have them, I wanted at the very least a tangible reminder of my proximity to them.

Suddenly my gut instinct shouted out so that I couldn't ignore it. I knew, in that mystical sense of "knowing" what we cannot rationally know, that it would be wrong for me to remove anything from that circle of stones. I should *leave* something, rather than *take* something.

Well, now, this was a novel idea. I was used to consumer travel. Why, I had even "stolen" a piece of rock from the Irish-Catholic cemetery where my husband's ancestors had been buried. He doesn't even know yet. I justified this defiling act (which basically I deplore) by my plan to turn it into an "art" object of some sort and present it to him on some future date as a gift from his root-land. I'm great at such justifications. I employ them in all sorts of settings and on all sorts of occasions—commercial or otherwise.

Yet, suddenly, standing there in the midst of the circle of stones, I couldn't do it, even though I longed to. I couldn't take anything—not even a leaf. I worried for a moment that my hubby's camera was "taking" images to which we were not entitled, but then I decided (sometimes I *can* be practical) that Dan was taking them, not I, and that it was his responsibility, not mine, whether or not it was a "right" action. Besides, he's Irish. The fairies probably wouldn't mind a bit.

So, I looked for something to leave. I looked in my purse and pockets for something adequate, but found nothing. I finally left a self-conscious song and an equally self-conscious (though totally silent) prayer.

It wasn't until much later that I realized I had left empty-handed but not ungifted. I had received a metaphor: for some things, it is profoundly preferable to *leave* something rather than to *take* something. It occurred to me that this is how I should approach many things, indeed, perhaps life itself.

It also occurred to me that this was not exactly an entirely original notion. Nonetheless, it was the first time I had ever experienced the metaphor this concretely, so to speak. Perhaps the word is "religiously." In any case, the whole event spoke to me loudly.

Home

God gives the desolate a home to dwell in...   Psalm 68:6

We all know desolate people. They're the ones we read about in the headlines who, somehow, have gotten their lives so out of whack that they rob and shoot innocent victims. They're the prisoners huddled in their cells, too frightened to venture outside for their daily exercise. They're the teenagers with slash marks on their wrists, trapped in a mental vice they don't know how to discard. They're the welfare recipients who are stuck in a system that keeps them unemployed and/or unemployable. They're the next-door neighbors who don't vote because what difference does it make anyway? They're the young black men and women who move away from the neighborhood they've called home all their lives because they're afraid that the next drive-by shooting will hit their ten year-old child playing outside in the street. They're the white suburbanites who refuse to live in the city because it's too dangerous. They're the walkers who cross over to the other side of the street when they see someone who looks suspicious. They're the old folks at the movies who won't say anything to the obnoxiously noisy teens in the row behind them because "you just don't know what might happen these days." They're the middle-aged couple who just found out he has pancreatic cancer, and that it's already spread to the liver.

Who are these desolate people? They are we. We are the desolate people, whether we recognize it or not. We are the lonely, the forlorn, the hopeless. Oh, not all of us all of the time, certainly. But all of us, some of the time.

And why are we desolate? Depending on your viewpoint, there may be several answers to this question, at least several different theological answers. Some say we are born sinners, and hence we are desolate by definition. Some hold that while we aren't born sinners, we all sin, and hence our desolation stems from our actions. Others say we are simply imperfect creatures, and hence our desolation is an inevitable part of our humanness. Still others believe we are born to a cycle of suffering, desolation our inevitable karma until blessed death releases us. My personal perspective is that we are born to experience the world of limitation, and the frustrations of not understanding this limitation give rise to our sense of desolation.

But, whatever the perspective, I maintain that *we* are the ones whom the Psalmist addressed when he asserted that "God gives the desolate a home to dwell in." God gives *us* a home to dwell in, call it…well, what do we call our home?

There are, I believe, two fundamental answers to this question, and, although they are different answers, I suggest that they are also one and the same. What is our home? Easy: it is Earth. Our home is Earth. Clearly, our home is Earth. But it is not just the Earth which the astronauts see from afar as a roundish blue ball. Nor is it only the Earth that the environmentalists worry over. Nor is it merely the rich, moist dirt that the farmer spins into golden harvests. Rather, Earth is more like a mental hospital, a place of care and healing, a place of refuge and challenge, a place filled with crazy, desolate individuals, torn by their separateness. The Earth is a *Richard Young Memorial Universe:*[2]

> *The key turns at birth. The door behind us*
> *plainly announces: No one leaves*
> *until they are ready. Besides,*
> *Special Care is filled with lush greenery,*
> *donated newspapers, three*
> *dimensions. You've got to wonder*
> *how much all this hope costs*
> *and who pays, anyway? Thank them,*
> *somebody, it's nice to be held! 'Course*

I don't understand why I am here
or what makes the door buzz open
or why the windows hint so loudly,
so unremittingly
I am my own keeper.
I am my own keeper.
I am my own keeper.

Earth is a Special Care unit for desolate folk. For us. It's a place where (unless we mess up) we all have the basics, such as food and shelter. It's a place with the security of a predictable schedule. The sun rises every morning and sets every evening day after day after day, and the days fall into a pattern of spring, summer, fall, winter, year after year after year. This cycle offers so much security that we make calendar-renditions of it and we plan our daily lives down to the minute on the basis of this pre-dictability.

Our home Earth offers more than food, shelter, predictability. In it, we are assured of a few fundamental rules and responsibilities. Eat up all the food resources, and everyone suffers. Replenish what you harvest and take care of what you plant. You reap what you sow. Do not kill. Do not commit adultery. Do not steal. Do not bear false witness. Do not defraud. Honor your father and mother. The rules of this home are really pretty few and pretty simple, and we all basically agree on them, even if we don't always seek them out, as I just did in Exodus 20.

Likewise, Earth offers us boundaries which allow respect for private turf. Mountains separate countries, rivers separate states, forests shield actions and night darkness creates a privacy we take for granted. As for providing us opportunity to respect legitimate authority…who among us will argue with a tornado or a snowstorm? Who will not submit to the demands of a harsh growing season, or the pleasures of a sunny spring day? Mother Nature provides a voice of authority that only the daft fail to respect and to honor.

Earth is a place where our five developmental needs (the basics such as shelter and food, the security of a predictable schedule, a few agreed upon rules and responsibilities, boundaries that govern respect for private turf, and respect for legitimate authority), and our five relational needs (care, honesty and objectivity, open communication of feelings, tolerance of negative or ambiguous feelings, respect for the body), and any other needs we don't even know about, can be met. It's a marvelous place, filled with potential for the healing of broken spirits and the enrichment of limited souls.

God gives the desolate a home to dwell in, and the name of that home is Earth. Earth is the way textbooks and secular humanists and geographers and poets and artists and sometimes preachers describe our home. But the mystics among us give it a different name. To the mystic, God gives the desolate a home to dwell in, and the name of that home is Faith.

The Home of Faith provides for our needs. The Psalmist remembers that "Thou hast been a shelter for me." (Psalm 61:3) Paul reminds us that it is in Faith that we find shelter and food (Romans 14:17-23), and he advises us of the subtle and intricate connection between Faith and Earthly provisions: "For we brought nothing into this world, and it is certain we can carry nothing out. And having food and raiment let us be therewith content." (1 Timothy 6:7-8)

Similarly, there are rules and responsibilities in this House of Faith: the "righteous shall live by faith." (Romans 1:17) There is predictability in faith: "…if you have faith as a grain of mustard seed, you will say to this mountain, 'Move from here to there,' and it will move; and nothing will be impossible to you." (Matthew 17:20) There is respect for legitimate authority: "The promise of Abraham and his descendants, that they should inherit the world, did not come through the law but through the righteousness of faith." (Romans 4:13) There are even boundaries and respect for private turf in the Home of Faith. Consider, for example, how discreetly the apostles acted: "And when they had come opposite Mysia, they attempted to go into Bithynia, but the Spirit of Jesus did not allow them…." (Acts 16: 6-7) It is in the House of Faith that, ultimately, we find peace, nurture, salvation: "For by grace you have been saved *through faith* (emphasis added); and this is not your own doing, it is the gift of God." (Ephesians 2:8)

Earth offers us a home where our needs, developmental or otherwise, can be met. Faith offers us such a home as well. Faith and Earth are two different ways of viewing the same home. One is totally sense-oriented, dependent upon our physical touch, sight, hearing, etc. The other is totally *non*-sense-oriented. Some even call it nonsense, because this view lends itself to the non-ordinary—to faith-healing, miracles, Red Seas opening up, etc. But those who call it nonsense do so misguidedly for the House of Faith is built deep within our hearts, where we experience it at will even though our eyes can never see it.

When perceived from the heart of a mystic, Faith is the place which Jesus tells us about, the place where "now they know that everything that thou hast given me is from thee." (John 17:7) Faith is the place where our souls are both tested and nurtured, and where those who are hopeless find renewal. Faith is the place that stretches our minds and opens us to new ways of interaction. Faith is the home where the desolate speak in tongues, and no one laughs or shames. Faith is the one address where we all know and enjoy certain *Inalienable Freedoms:*[3]

To smile
to greet people with respect
to be true to yourself
to die glad you lived
to trust

To choose your
thoughts your parents
your present your
past, future

To exist in linear time,
Human,

aware

that stones speak
the same earth language
and even butterflies
pray.

Dialogue

I f the earth could talk, what do you suppose she would say to us? Here are some suggestions.

Possibility ① *You just don't dig it!* It's *your* acts that are killing me. Your automobiles. Your toxic waste. Your acid rain. Your over-population. I could go on and on, humans, but I am only a small planet, and I am struggling too much to more than rumble. Out of my dust you arose, but never before have any of the species living on me had the capacity to destroy themselves in a few hours and to ruin most of my life-support systems in the process. Never before has a species engaged in action that could totally destroy my delicate ecological balance in a "gradual" manner taking less than a century. Ouch, folks, you're hurting me.

Possibility ② *Water, water everywhere, but, thanks to you, none that's fair. And more.* Did you know, humans, that it takes an entire forest—over 500,000 trees—to supply Americans with their Sunday newspapers every week?[4] Did you know that when you toss out one aluminum can you waste as much energy as if you'd filled the same can half full of gasoline and poured it on the ground? Did you know that every year Americans throw away 18 billion disposable diapers—enough to stretch to the moon and back seven times? Did you know that you can easily use more than 5 gallons of water if you leave the tap running while you brush your teeth? Did you know that it takes a barrel of crude oil to produce the rubber on a truck tire? Did you know that a U.S. Fish and Wildlife survey of albatross babies found 90% with plastic in their digestive system? Please, please, don't take me for granted.

Possibility ③ *Everything you ever needed to know you were taught in kindergarten, but you just didn't seem to listen!* Since you humans first appeared on my surface a few million years ago, you have changed me considerably. You're as clever as any creatures I've seen. Why, you've created entirely new environments for yourselves—farms, villages, towns, crowded cities, ocean liners, underwater dwellings. You've changed me to fit you.

But part of you hasn't changed as much as I have. In particular, the brain part hasn't changed much. A long time ago, your ancestors used their brain power primarily to do things that required quick responses to threats that were immediate, personal, and palpable—an unexpected encounter with a giant cave bear, a stroke of lightning, a thrown spear. Today, you use your brain power in just the same way. If a child runs in front of your car, you slam on the brakes almost without thinking about it. An unexpected encounter with a burglar alerts you and gets the brain juices running.

Yet, today you have other threats, threats which are gradual, often impersonal, and sometimes impalpable. These threats require a different type of response. They are threats which were generated by complex technological devices developed by people living half a world away and perhaps half a century ago. They are threats like the gradual buildup of nuclear arms, the slow atmospheric accumulation of carbon dioxide, the almost imperceptible depletion of the ozone layer. Your nervous systems seem to be programmed for dramatic changes, and you tend to ignore those that are slow and subtle. One atomic explosion over Hiroshima makes a far greater impression than the vaster but less dramatic destruction of Tokyo by conventional incendiary bombs. A single airplane crash or the plight of one little girl trapped in a well commands your attention more than the expansive threat to life of gradual population overgrowth.[5]

Humans, no longer need you see me only from the narrow perspective of your toes digging into my soil. Now you can see me from the wide view of outer space. I am the third planet from your sun. I am a little planet, small enough that you can encircle me in about an hour with gadgets you've made. I am a blue planet, filled with spirit-giving water. And I talk. I talk in a voice that can't be heard immediately or personally. You can hear me easiest when you least expect…

—when you are farthest from me or when you are littlest.

—when you are told, as Robert Fulghum told in his well-known book,[6] "Share everything. Play fair. Don't hit people. Put things back where you found them. Clean up your own mess."

—when you are told, "Remember the little seed in the plastic cup. The roots go down and the plant goes up and nobody really knows how or why, but we are all like that."

Oh yes, I do, indeed, have a voice. Why, oh, why aren't you listening?

Possibility ④ *Hey, folks, you need me more than I need you.* It may be hard to believe, but it's true. Not that I don't like you, but, well, let's be realistic. If you compress my history into a single calendar year, with midnight January 1 being my birth and midnight December 31st being the present, then dinosaurs arrived around December 10th, disappeared on Christmas day, and the first recognizable human ancestors appeared sometime on the afternoon of December 31st. You humans came about 11:45 p.m.

It's true, we have a nice little ecosystem going. I am clothed in a blanket of carbon dioxide. Since it keeps me warm, I try to take care of it. I work hard to keep the amount of carbon in the air, in the sea, and on the land relatively constant. You fit nicely into this carbon-blanket system. You breathe it out, plants take it in—that sort of thing. I have to watch this blanket pretty carefully, though. Without it, I'd be about twenty degrees colder than I am. If you think that's healthy, try it yourselves! On the other hand, if my blanket grows, it might get too hot. Look what happened to Venus! If you're a planet like me, I tell you it's a scary prospect.

I've seen a lot of species come and go in my life and, while I'm not exactly threatening you, I think it's the sort of fact you ought to be aware of. To be honest, you seem to be messing up my eco-blanket these days. I don't need this, humans. I don't want this. I don't think you can get along without me, but I sure as heck can get along without you. You need me, folks. You need me more than I need you.

Possibility ⑤ *When I grow up, I want to be alive, too!* To be *really* honest, I'm not so all-fired sure of that last statement—the one about you needing me more than I need you. It's funny, but nothing's had the same effect on me that you've had. You're creative. You're inventive. You've got all this, this raw potential. When you're not abusing me, I pretty much like you.

The thing is, there seems to be something else going on here, something not only bigger than you, but bigger than me as well. It's crazy, but there's a kind of order about this whole thing that even I can't fully understand. I know that some of you humans seem to be sympathetic to this order—and to me. Many of you call me Gaia and recognize the fact that I am alive. But, I am still a youngster, folks. I want to grow up and be alive.

Possibility ⑥ *I'm afraid!* In spite of my bravado, I don't really know where we're going. I'm not really sure that you could disappear without taking me with you. I am fascinated by you, delighted by you, intrigued by you. Yet, I am also afraid of you, of your power. I don't want to be contaminated. I don't want to be a wasteland. I don't want to die until I have fully lived.

Possibility ⑦ *God help me. God help us all!*

Choice

I dreamt about you last night, agency lady, and woke up grumbling.

"That goody-goody social worker," I said to Mark. Where's she get off, judging us like that?

Mark rolled his eyes at me. He didn't comment.

"What gives her the right?" I persisted, staring impatiently at the knotted hump still lazing in bed.

"I should know, Joyce," he snarled.

I was tempted to snarl back, but I knew he was upset, too, and besides, if we had rehashed yesterday's interview before breakfast, what with Mark being so ultra-slow, he'd almost certainly be late for work. Resignedly, I lumbered off to the kitchen, plugged in the coffeepot, and set the table for two. Two, when there should have been three or four or more, except for some opinionated agency lady who didn't feel we qualified as potential adoptive parents. Only two, agency lady, because of you.

Nine years it's been and I'm over forty now. Nine years of forms and references and convincing. Nine years on the waiting list and for what? Yesterday's "a slight possibility we might be able to place a handicapped child with you, Mrs. Green."

You burned me up, agency lady, with your undersized nose and your plucked eyebrows and your patronizing voice. And I burn the toast there in the kitchen this morning just thinking about you, which burns Mark until we finally start snarling and he has to catch a second bus into the city after all.

You clung to me all day, shadowing me even as I hurried through my morning chores. "Naturally, I do all my own housework," I'd told you only hours ago. "I do the cooking, the ironing, the cleaning. I do it all." I had gestured, inviting you to examine my livingroom, the windowsills, under the bed. You merely sat there on my rose slip-covered couch which I had laundered just for your visit, sat there, with your sharpened pencil and your pointed eyebrows, saying, "Perhaps you don't realize how physically demanding an infant can be."

Well, little miss arched eyes, my brows may not be as neatly manicured as yours, nor my face as dainty, but I'll wager one year of my earnings at the Center that I can out-swim you any day of the week. Would you rather share a session with me on the hand-bars? How about a snappy game of table tennis? I'll take you on sitting down and spot you ten.

You can't, eh! Might hurt that precious back you had the nerve to complain to me about. It slays me. My back hurts, too. My back and my head and plenty of other spots, but I don't go telling the world. My Aunt Marge does that. And my neighbor two houses down. But Mark and I never toss complaints, not even to each other.

I told Ginny Adams, three houses up and across the street, about you when I went at eleven to babysit Kenneth. I adore Kenneth—his Mamajoyce, he calls me—but today I came close to agreeing with you, agency lady. My God, that child is active. I finally had to put a harness on him and, really, we got along fine after that. He makes mincemeat of Ginny, though—into this and into that and making her chase him all over the place. He'd holler fits if *she* ever tied him down, but with me…. Funny, how kids adjust.

"Hawsey," Kenneth begged me. "Pway hawsey, Mamajoyce." He tried to climb up on my lap.

"Joyce doesn't play horsey like that," I told him firmly. "You get down on all fours, and I'll scoot down, and we'll both be horses in the field, okay? Show me what a good horsy you can be, Kenneth."

"You Mama Hawsey," he said, and that was all there was to it. It's only social workers and the like who can't budge the rules.

"How can that social worker be so heartless?" Ginny asked when she returned from her luncheon. "You and Mark of all people have so much love to give a child. That woman is either stupid or crazy or both."

"Maybe we're the ones who are stupid or crazy. We should have tried to have our own child when we were still young enough to consider it."

"Oh, come on, Joyce. You know how risky the doctor said it was."

"Yeah, so now I'm past forty and childless and that social witch says I don't have enough stamina left to be a full-time mother."

I'd probably have rattled on endlessly if it hadn't been for the Center, but I'm expected there two to five daily, so I hugged Kenneth, made my way clumsily to the bus stop at the end of the lane, and spent the next three hours trying to give hope to the seven handicapped youngsters I see every weekday. "Give people a chance," I tell them relentlessly, "and they will give you a chance." Only this afternoon I stumbled over the words just as they stumbled with their awkward limbs, and I left precisely at five on a real downer.

Ah, agency lady! I don't have the endurance for a healthy child, you say, but would I consider one with an impairment? That takes less energy, I ask? You should be with me from two to five every day.

I did a few laps at the indoor pool on my way home, but somehow the water didn't wash away yesterday's wounds. You were with me even as I unlocked our front door—yes, social worker, we do own our own home. You were with me as I emptied the stew from the crock pot onto our plates, and with me as we emptied our plates and emptied the dishwasher. Mark read the evening paper aloud while I tidied the kitchen—our nightly ritual done so often we almost take it for granted. Almost. Always, almost. Strange, how many people assume that since I wear spectacles I can see perfectly. People assume so much. You, agency lady, you assume so much, and you judge on your assumptions.

Mark and I didn't broach the adoption again, mainly because it was our Friday night for bridge and we had to scurry so that we'd be ready when the Robinsons picked us up. Even the cards were against us today. We couldn't seem to bid right or play right and once Mark knocked over his card holder, which always embarrasses him, and then he accidentally bumped the tea cup, spilling it all over the Eckleys' tablecloth.

Worse yet, there was one couple substituting for the Brachs, and the woman—she looked remarkably like you, agency lady, same plucked eyebrows and all—anyway, she simply couldn't seem to understand anything Mark said, kept asking him to repeat it, only slower please.

"Okay, so we ought to be used to it by now," Mark muttered as he undressed for bed. I felt bad because he felt bad, which, when you get right down to it, is one of the nice things about the way it is with Mark and me. Heaven only knows, we're not picture-people, Mark with his cerebral palsy and me with my deformed half-legs sticking out of braces. Mark and I, we've overcome plenty of obstacles. Yet, there's always more. More agency ladies to overcome.

Sure, social worker, I should have phoned you tonight. "Yes," I should have said. "Yes, certainly Mark and I want a handicapped child." But I lost heart for the words. Maybe tomorrow I'll call, but not tonight. Tonight I'm tired. Tonight I want only bed, bed and dreamless sleep.

Probability

To see things in the seed, that is genius. Lao-Tzu

What is the probability that an essay on statistics and hope belongs in this collection? If you say "zero," I urge you to read on.

Statistics is what I used to teach to one of my classes. (Some of my students called it "sadistics.") Statistics deals with hard facts. It crunches numbers out of elaborate, sometimes mind-boggling equations and spits out expectations in the form of probabilities. Statistics isn't particularly easy. But, then, neither is hope. Hope is what I try to experience in my ministry. Hope deals with soft facts. Hope crunches courage out of disappointments and setbacks, and it spits out expectations in the form of faith. On the whole, finding hope is a much more demanding challenge than learning statistics, even sadistic statistics. There is, after all, so much to be discouraged about in this life.

I'd like to say hope is what I teach in my ministry, but somehow that seems a bit presumptuous since I'm still learning hope, myself. Rest assured, I know about the struggle for hope. Depression forces you to look for hope in places where you might least expect to find it. Prayer, church, therapy, medication, even supporting legislation to further research on certain diseases…I've tried them all. Some have helped. But when you're in need of hope, it pays to be inventive in your search. So the mathematician in me turned to statistics for hope. I found in statistics a hope I had not anticipated.

First, statistics brings us new perspective, something essential to those who are without hope. Sometimes our problems seem so overwhelming that we feel impotent and helpless in the face of them. Currently the world seems to be riding a rapid road to disaster. Even the size of the human population presents a problem. Did you know that of all the people who have ever lived on earth, over half of them have lived during *this* century? That's a lot of people. It's hard enough to get a sense of such a big number, let alone feel that we're anything but one more insignificant, faceless creature in a vast impersonal sea. I couldn't do it until I'd read a statistical summary by Donella Meadows called "If the World Were a Village of 1,000 People."[7] If the world were a village of 1,000 people, it would include 584 Asians, 124 Africans, 95 eastern and western Europeans—that sort of thing.

With the aid of statistics, suddenly we dwell in a village. We can relate to a village. In a village, we can really grasp what is going on. Better yet, in a village, we have an identity. We *are* somebody. We make a difference. In a village, it matters what one person does. Why, if only one more person becomes a doctor in our village of 1000, suddenly the number of doctors has doubled. If *you* become a doctor, *you* make a 200% difference in the quality of health care. See what I mean? With statistics we can change our perspective and, in the process, recognize that we are not so powerless as we thought. This is the makings of hope.

Second, statistics can suggest avenues of action. People who are afraid they might lose their jobs are better off if they use control (problem-focused) rather than escape (emotion-focused) coping strategies. Men who suffer a head injury—in childhood or afterward—may be at risk of becoming aggressive toward their partner and, hence, might consider preventive positive action, namely, premarital counseling. Early detection of birth complications may help prevent violent crimes later on. There is hope in these and similar statistical findings.[8]

In the process of reshaping our perspectives and offering guidance regarding our best paths of action, statistics often provides us much-needed reassurance and encouragement. You may not be especially surprised at the scientific studies which conclude that the pursuit of happiness involves 1) an ability to adapt to changing circumstances, 2) a view of the world as benevolent and controllable, and 3) values and goals that provide a sense of direction.[9] Yet, chances are, you'll be at least a little reassured. Happiness really is attainable: just concentrate on these three factors.

The statistics of encouragement can be quite subtle. For instance, one recent *Newsweek*[10] carried a report of an elegant study concluding that Alzheimer's disease may be more frequent among those who demonstrate something called "low idea density" and "grammatical complexity." Specifically, if your writing style is dense and complex, you may have some sort of built-in resistance to encroaching dementia. In my own personal family history, Alzheimer's has sometimes been a problem. So, if you think that this essay is too difficult and convoluted to follow, how can I help but be encouraged?

And here's one more item I ran across not long ago which, I admit, has already provided me with an inordinate amount of reassurance and encouragement. The title tells it all: "Whiners May Be Better Off, Study Finds."[11] "Go ahead and complain," invited the article. "Whine if you must. Expressing your discontent could help you live longer than your quiet, inner-suffering pals."

Furthermore, according to another study,[12] "People whose religious beliefs give them feelings of strength and comfort and who regularly participate in a social activity markedly improve their chance of surviving at least 6 months after undergoing heart surgery…." This last illustration points to a fact so significant, at least from my standpoint as a minister, that I think it

warrants being counted as a separate way in which statistics can help us find hope. In particular, *statistics* suggest that we enhance our religious commitment. The *Wall Street Journal*[13] points out that "the potential of churches and synagogues to improve the quality of health care in America has made 'Congregation-Based Health Ministry' the hottest topic within virtually all the denominations of every religion." Still another report says it even more succinctly: "For Good Health, Go to Church." As a group, religious folk live longer than non-religious folk and, in addition to lengthening your life, religion can actually lower your chances of getting sick. Infrequent religious attendance, warn these researchers, "should be regarded as a consistent risk factor for morbidity and mortality of various types."[14] Now, as a minister wanting to minister, these statistics give me hope!

Yes, statistics convince. Today, we look to statistics for truth with a Platonic faith that mathematical reality is the ultimate reality—more real, to some, than God. Two plus two is four. Period. The truth, the absolute truth and nothing but the truth. In a study titled "The Impact of Religion on Man's Blood Pressure," psychiatrist and former National Institute of Mental Health researcher David Larsen determined that, statistically speaking, "even smokers benefit from religion."[15] Truth. Absolute truth. Statistics convince. Yet, somehow we suspect that these same statistics can be used to mislead, to delude, to lie. Statistics may give us truth, but can we *trust* it? What a paradox of thought we have here!

Edward MacNeal, in *Mathsemantics*,[16] relates how he asked 196 job applicants to solve the following addition problem: What is the sum of two apples and five oranges? Fifty-two applicants answered "7 fruit." Forty-six answered "7." Just seven, not seven of anything. Thirty-six answered "2 apples + 5 oranges," which, MacNeal allowed, didn't seem to solve any problem in addition. Twenty-seven applicants refused to "add unlike values." Fifteen responded "7 apples and oranges," fifteen waffled, and five gave clearcut wrong answers such as "7 oranges." All in all, the 196 applicants answering the question gave 56 digitally different responses. Now, how the heck can anyone find hope in the mathematics of such a slippery process?

What MacNeal is getting at is the notion that there is nothing wrong with our mathematics—it's our math *semantics* that cause us difficulties. If I hold up a red pencil and a green pencil and ask you to add them, chances are you'll say "two pencils. "But, no," I say. "This is a reddie and this is a greenie. You can't add greenies and reddies."

"But they're both pencils," you protest.

"So," says MacNeal, "whether you can add things together depends on what they're called, is that right? If I call them 'fruit,' you can add them together, but if I call them 'apples' and 'oranges,' you can't. That makes it a question of who will do the naming, doesn't it?"

Traditional schooling, contends MacNeal, does little to put math and semantics together and hence to address the seeming problem. Instead it yields adults who are afraid to use numbers, who fear that "math is a powerful mystery they're not privileged to know." This mystery creates a chasm which, for many adults, becomes a hopeless pit. "Math anxiety" is one term frequently used to define the condition. "Escapist coping" is perhaps more accurate.

Let me illustrate with another example from MacNeal's book. Here's a little test for you. What year do you think the capital of Burma was founded? I'd like you to answer this. In fact, I'd like you to *tell* your answer to someone else. Some of you may be uncomfortable with this little exercise. Some of you may argue that, heck, you don't even know what the capital of Burma is, let alone when it was founded.[17] Some of you may even refuse to give an answer. If so, you are among the majority. Most people, MacNeal discovered, refuse to make an estimate. They fear being wrong.

Such fear impedes our knowledge acquisition by discouraging what MacNeal calls our least expensive and most valuable learning technique—trial and error. I believe he is right. But I also believe he has held up for us to see a valuable lesson for all of us who quest after hope.

In order to enjoy hope, we have to be willing to risk something. In particular, we have to be willing to risk being wrong, to risk failing. R.H. Macy failed seven times before his now-famous store in New York caught on. English novelist John Creasey acquired 753 rejection slips before he published 564 books. Babe Ruth struck out 1,330 times, yet he also hit 714 home runs. Abraham Lincoln was defeated for public office four times, failed in business, couldn't get into law school, went bankrupt, lost his fiancee to death, had a total nervous breakdown and was in bed for six months, and received fewer than 100 votes when he sought the Vice-Presidential nomination at his party's national convention. Lincoln didn't let failure stop him. He took a chance. And then another and another.[18]

The most valuable lesson we can glean about hope from statistics is that statistics is all about probabilities—about chance. Consider a carton of ordinary sunflower seeds. Each one of these seeds is a miniature math program. We can read about such programs in chemistry and biology texts where they are typically called "genetic coding." If we plant one of these seeds, we have a good sense of the probable outcome—especially if we water and nurture it. It is not a certainty that this seed will produce a brilliant sunflower. But the chances are pretty good.

Whenever we plant a seed like this, or any seed, we are taking a chance. We are risking. We are trusting in probabilities and statistics. What we reap, ultimately, is hope. Take a chance today. Plant a seed. Grow hope.

Fences

I say why? Sure, some hold in, protect.
Some even look pretty. On farms, fences
frequently hold barbs and electric charges.
When you are small and brave, you test
such fences with wet grass: the shock
reverberates down the line of your life, never
letting you forget that fences function first
to separate and bite.

When I moved to Chicago's Hyde Park, I discovered a new kind of fence, a zero-fence. It's an invisible fence, but it separates and bites even more bitterly than the fence you can touch. You can't tear it down easily, because you can't see it.

Even invisible, everybody knows it's there. In Hyde Park this fence runs roughly from Lake Michigan along 47th Street until it reaches Cottage Grove Avenue, where it turns south to the Midway and then east again back to the lake. It corrals a bunch of middle-class people—all colors, mostly well-off, mostly intelligent—something like we fenced our dairy cattle into lush pastures back on the farm. It separates them (or tries to) from the rest of Chicago's poor, mostly black, Southside just as effectively as our farm fence separated the cows from the corn field.

I spent about two decades on that farm, not quite a third of my life. On the farm I learned quite a lot about fences. Some fences are better than others. We used to have a snow fence that we put up and took down alongside the driveway seasonally: in winter it made the snows more manageable. As fences go, it was a pretty good little fence. Today I've come to understand that even some zero-fences can be fairly beneficial. Victims of domestic abuse, for instance, often need an invisible fence of self-esteem and determination before they can change their status from victim to survivor. But this fence in Hyde Park, and others like it throughout the world…well, they must make the angels cry.

If I've stomped on any toes in identifying the placement of this fence so precisely, I can only say that this is what I was *told* when I moved to Chicago. "Oh, Hyde Park is a wonderful place. You'll love it there. Safety? Well, it's probably better if you don't venture much beyond 47th Street or the Midway, or…." Granted, I probably already carried the makings of a zero-fence within me or I wouldn't have thought to ask that question about safety. On the other hand, where did that question come from in the first place? Do I hear the angels crying?

Some folks apparently think there's considerable misperception about just where those invisible boundaries around Hyde Park are placed. But then, that's what those invisible fences are really built of, isn't it? Misperceptions. Misperceptions stacked on top of each other as though they were concrete blocks. Why, you look at those misperceptions all set so closely together like that, and you'd think we weren't all of us in this life together. On one level, we all know better, but somehow those unseen, untouchable fences which segregate and elevate are real. They scare me more than the barbed-wire electric kind.

If only we'd listen, I'll bet those angels would tell us what to do about those unwanted, unnecessary fences. "Talk to each other," they might say. "Listen to each other. It's easier to hear each other than it is to hear us weeping. And when you start to listen, you start to see as well. There they are…big coiled barbs of zero, just waiting to be turned into something else."

Singing

Jesus, the great prophet, found no honor in his hometown. The folks who knew him best from childhood—the neighbor, the friend he played with, the cousin down the street, whoever—*these* were the ones who "took offense at him." But what can we of two thousand years later glean from his hometown rejection? After all, Jesus wasn't from *my* hometown up there in the northeastern corner of Ohio. He probably wasn't from *any* of our hometowns and, indeed, most of us probably haven't even *seen* that patch of land across the sea where Jesus was born. Clearly, *we* are apart from those few unfortunates who "took offense" at this upstart prophet, refusing him honor, respect, even simple credence.

Or are we apart?

This is a story about my youngest daughter Melinda. At the time of this story, Melinda was thirteen, and she and I were living in Chicago, where I was attending seminary. Our tiny apartment was a small nest up on the third and top floor of a building inhabited almost exclusively by other seminary students and their families.

It was about 8:30 p.m. Melinda and I were working away in our small apartment when suddenly Melinda announced that she was going outside in the hallway and would be back. As she shut the apartment door behind her, I could hear her singing down the corridor. Her voice was lovely: lilting, flowing, but, as I was busy studying, I paid it scant attention.

110

A little while later I heard the door open and Melinda disappeared into the tiny nook she used as her "office." Time passed. As I really was engrossed in my books, I was only vaguely aware that she was unusually silent. After a bit, she came quietly into my room and asked if I would read something. I looked at the folded pink stationery she held out to me. The look on her face told me that this was one of those times when I should set aside my studying. Her writing was painstakingly neat—the script carefully formed and the spelling and punctuation almost perfect:

> Ma'am,
> I am greatly sorry I annoyed you by my singing. I will be more considerate next time. However, the way you approached me

really stung. I wish you to know for your future as a minister because I think it is important.

I was outside in the hall practicing a difficult piece of music for a concert I will be performing soon, and I was trying to keep from distracting anyone below or beside me when you came out and asked, "Excuse me, what are you doing?" in a not so friendly tone. Astonished by your tone I said shyly, "Singing," and you replied even with a more harsh tone, "Well, it's very annoying."

I was amazed that someone studying for the ministry could be so outright mean. I hope that in the future you will be more considerate of other people's feelings when you are trying to comfort them or just tell them anything. Like, please, although you are practicing could you please go someplace like downstairs, because I am having a difficult time concentrating—this would have left me feeling better and with another alternative.

Thank you,
Melinda Voss.

I looked at the hurt young woman standing before me, obviously seeking what wisdom I had to offer, and my heart went out to her. There'd been a time, a time not so long before, when Melinda would have stomped angrily away, keeping her hurt buried deeply inside where neither of us could get at it. There was a time when she wouldn't have trusted me enough to share this letter, much less to ask my advice about it.

We talked about the letter and about her feelings. And about my feelings. I told her how proud I was of her to be trying to stick up for herself when she had been wronged. How hard it must have been for her to exercise enough self-control to write a response. How wonderful it felt that she trusted my judgment enough to come and ask me for my input. I gave her some suggestions for the letter. She accepted every one of them, went back to her nook, edited out the accusatory parts and added a few more "I feels." When it was done, it was a letter any adult could have been proud to have written. When I pointed out, cautiously, that maybe going down the hall singing loudly had been distracting to the people who were not "below" her or "beside" her, she replied with a little laugh, "Oh, yes, I shouldn't have done it." Her ability to accept responsibility for her actions, her willingness to work through her feelings, and her ability to begin to put herself in the other person's position astounded me. This was a Melinda I had not seen before.

She took the letter down the hall, knocked on the door, and gave the annoyed neighbor her letter. When she returned, she was beaming. "She was *nice*, Mom." We went to bed that night feeling good about each other, about ourselves, and about the whole incident. In the morning, there was a wonderful note under the door for Melinda from the woman down the hall apologizing for *her* acid response and Melinda's right to be upset. Melinda, she wrote, had taught *her* a valuable lesson about being more sensitive.

There are a lot of warm fuzzies in this story, not the least of which is that Melinda was willing to let me put this story into a book. I know that both my daughter and I handled a tough situation in a positive way. At one time, neither one of us would have been able to do that! To be honest, we haven't always been able to do it since then, either, but our efforts today are inevitably affected, positively affected, by the success we had on this one occasion years ago.

Yet, although I enjoy these warm fuzzies, there are two main messages that I particularly want to lift up out of this story. First, **I** almost cut off Melinda's singing. I was the main person who was "beside" Melinda. It was my studying that she was trying not to disturb in the first place. Now, I don't sing much around the house these days. Perhaps I never did. Yet the sound of Melinda's voice singing is one of the things I cherish in life. It is one of the things that makes it all worth while, and I don't want her to stop. How many times do I, does the neighbor down the hall, how many times do we all unthinkingly cut off the singing? How many times are we so busy that we don't even hear the songs in life?

I, for one, don't want that to happen again.

The second message is that Melinda, in her own way, was a "little" prophet for me, and for the neighbor down the hall as well. She had something to teach us, something about having love and caring and honesty and basic respect for each other. Something about appreciating the joy in life. Yet Melinda was the one I lived with all the time. She is my "hometowner." How easy it is for me, for all of us, to ignore the wisdom of these "little" prophets who live with us daily.

I, for one, don't want *that* to happen anymore, either.

How easy it is for us to be so engrossed in our studying, or our businesses or our illnesses, or whatever, to be so engrossed in our own concerns and in our own little worlds that we simply shut out the important voices of those closest to us. This, I believe, is what Jesus' message is for us yet today. It is in our hometowns, among our own relatives and our own houses, that we still cut off the singing of our "prophets." So often our prophets today are right there in the room next to us, or down the hall. Would that we might make the effort to look for them, to listen to their wisdom, and to welcome their songs.

Rainbows

Everything was settled. We would move our aging mother to another care facility in another city. We all agreed. The tickets were purchased. The room was available. The city was mine.

"Please, God, let this be a wise move," I prayed, thinking of all the statistics about how hard a move was on the elderly. "Please, God, help me to find the strength and patience I need to get through this move and to care well for my mother."

It was a good, if brief prayer. At least, it was good enough. I was sincere. I was also, now that the actual arrangements had been made, just a little scared. We had been talking for months about the possibility of making this move. I was the one who had pushed for it to happen. Had I been correct to do so? Would I be able to live up to my own expectations in providing for my

mother in her last years? What if there weren't years? What if there were only days because of the move I had fostered? What if Mother was miserable and bitter and, worse, what if I couldn't fix her miserableness and bitterness? Self-doubt began to overwhelm me. "Please, God, I need some reassurance. Badly, God. I need reassurance badly."

How could God turn away from such a plea? All I was asking for was a bit of reinforcement. That was God's job, wasn't it? I grew a little self-right-eous. God was *supposed* to answer such prayers. I was trying to do the best I could for my mother. Honor thy mother. The least God could do was to help me.

Then the phone call came. Some of the family had changed their minds. At this late date, some of the family had decided that our agreed upon plan needed to be tossed. They brought up issues that we had already worked through, and here we were having to work them through all over again. For goodness sake, Family, we've already bought the tickets!! I was stunned. Then I was irritated. Then I was angry. Then I was resolute. They couldn't do this. This wasn't fair to Mother. Or to me. Or to the care facility which was hold-ing her place without any additional payment. What was *wrong* with that Family? God, what was I going to do now? And, by the way, God, why didn't you answer my prayer?

Suddenly it dawned on me that I was stunned, irritated, angry, and res-olute, but I wasn't the least bit uncertain any longer. In a curious way, I was reassured of the correctness of my original decision. God *had* answered my prayer. In a *very* curious way, I thought. This was not the way I'd had in mind—the soft, gentle embrace, the family gathering around, telling me how good I was to take on this task, telling me that they appreciated my effort on Mother's behalf.

Hm, I thought. Wonder why God answered my prayer this way? Was there something else I was being offered through this answer? Was God trying to tell me something? Hm, I thought. Hm.

If truth be known, I was irritated at God, too. Jeepers, all I'd asked for was a bit of reassurance and instead I'd gotten a challenge, a lesson, a worry, a…

Oh! Suddenly it hit me. I'd gotten a rainbow. I just hadn't been able to see it at first.

Rainbows are like that, you know. They appear out of nothing. They appear when you expect them, and when you don't as well. I have seen rainbows in the sky, in a waterfall, coming out of a fire hydrant, streaming from a small glass hung in my window, and even in an indoor swimming pool. I've read about prisms and the refraction of light waves and such things, but these scientific explanations, while interesting, don't capture the essence of a rainbow. Rainbows are ethereal and awe-inspiring, gorgeous and uncontainable, real and yet transient. Rainbows appear to consist of nothing, or at least nothing other than light, but whether or not we experience them depends, literally, upon our perspective at the time.

I think this is the way it is with prayer as well. Rainbows come out of prayer, too. Oh, not all the time. Some prayers don't bring rainbows, just as some rains don't bring them. Occasionally, though, you just get a beauty!

Apple Pie

Saturday night I called my twenty year-old daughter. She was making an apple pie. That is, she was trying to make an apple pie. She couldn't get the crust to hold together.

"What do I do, Mom?" she asked.

"Don't ask me." I shrugged my shoulders. I'm sure she saw the gesture even though she was fifty miles away and we were talking on the phone. "I never could make pies. I gave up trying a long time ago. My advice is to go out and buy a crust."

"It keeps crumbling," she complained, predictably ignoring my advice. Well, she hadn't asked for it, had she? That is, she had asked, but my advice wasn't the advice she wanted. "It won't roll out."

"You could try waxed paper," I offered lamely. "That's supposed to help."

"I don't have any waxed paper."

"Umm."

"I borrowed one of those things you have from a neighbor in the apartment across the way."

"Umm." That, of course, would have been my next suggestion. The "thing" she was referring to was a huge, flexible, white Tupperware sheet especially designed to make crust-making a breeze. It even had red markings on it to guide the rolling out of the dough. And very clear instructions as well. It sat in a drawer in my kitchen, unused for years except on the few occasions when my daughter, in her teenage years, had insisted on trying to bake a pie.

"I borrowed a roller, too. Oh, darn, I can't get it. Mom. Why didn't you teach me how to make pies?"

"Umm." My fault. "I don't know how," I replied quickly. "You know that." There was just an edge of exasperation in my tone. I'd had a bad day. "Some people just aren't pie-makers. It's like my ministry. No matter how hard I try, it just keeps crumbling."

This was an unfair comparison, I knew. As I said, though, I'd had a bad day. My ministry was a constant source of anguish for me. Currently, I was an "unsettled" minister, which meant I didn't have a church or any other official employment. I had watched my friends and colleagues go through seminary and walk into positions that seemed to work out perfectly, but, somehow, that never seemed to happen for me. Recently, I was tempted to stick my ministry in a drawer and forget about it. Some people just aren't pie-makers. The more I thought about it, the more I liked the metaphor.

My daughter, my youngest and the only one of my three children who had lived with me while I went through seminary eight years before, knew all about my hopes, dreams, and frustrations. She had an uncanny sense of how and when to deal with them. I owed her a lot. She kept me honest.

"I *have* to make this crust turn out," she continued, totally ignoring my ministerial plight. "I even borrowed the money to buy the ingredients. They're counting on me turning out a real pie."

"Just like my ministry," I tried again. I was thinking of the generous people who had put up money so long ago to help me through school. I hadn't wanted to let them down, either.

"I love you, Mom," my daughter said, and I smiled. I'm sure she saw the smile even though she was fifty miles away.

It occurred to me to wonder why my daughter, who lived in her own apartment and had recently decided to go back to college and try to finish, was baking a pie at ten-thirty on a Saturday night. "Sabina, NO!" Her voice came sharply over the phone. I could picture my daughter standing at the kitchen table, her hands messy with pie dough, trying to keep Sabina off the table. Sabina was her new kitten. I had warned her about kitty-adolescence. I had also warned her how a cat would tie her down just now and did she really need one? I wasn't sure she should have a cat until she finished school. But then, I wasn't sure about the two expensive birds she'd purchased a year ago either. Or that she should cut classes or travel across country by herself or date black men. My daughter never paid any attention to my uncertainties. I was proud of her.

"Oh, Mom, why didn't you ever teach me how to make pie crusts. How come *you* never learned?"

"Mother never taught me," I replied, truthfully. I knew about passing the buck.

"Why not? Couldn't she make pies either?"

My daughter was growing up, I realized. She was starting to put it all together, the way you do when you grow up and get insight.

"Oh, no. Grandma made wonderful pies." My mind flashed back to the farm and me as a little girl standing on a chair, peering over the high kitchen counter, my long blond curls hanging over my eyes, watching my mother expertly roll out the pie dough.

"Well, why didn't she teach you?"

"I don't know," I said, honestly baffled. "I was the last one. She probably didn't have the energy or time. Like me with you. No," I corrected myself. "That's not quite right. I didn't teach you because I didn't know how to make pies myself." There were plenty of things that I hadn't done for my youngest child because I didn't have the energy or time, but teaching her to make pies wasn't one of them. No sense in taking on unwarranted guilt. Sometimes I had "insight" myself.

"Did Aunt Mary Lynn make pies?"

I was impressed. My daughter *really* was searching for insight. "Yes," I said. "She made wonderful pies, too." For a moment, I missed my older sister with an ache. She had died some months ago. I wished now that I had told her how envious I was about her cooking skills. For a moment, I even wished I had asked her to teach me how to make good pie crust. In sixty years, well, no fifty years, that was really all the time I had with her, surely there would have been some time when we lived close enough together that I could have learned this culinary skill from her.

"Umm," my daughter said.

"Some people just are natural pie-makers," I added, again rather lamely.

"Umm."

I thought about reminding my youngest daughter that *her* older sister didn't cook anything at all, but then I decided that might reflect poorly on my own mothering skills, especially since I supposedly had time and energy for my oldest daughter. There are some things it's better not to say.

"Some people just can't make pies," I rephrased.

"Umm."

"Some people just can't make ministries." As I said, I'd had a bad day.

"Umm."

"Listen," I said. "I love you, too. Buy a crust. Or, there's a recipe for one you make out of crumbled cookies. I've got it somewhere. I've used it."

"Umm." In the background I could hear my daughter running water in her kitchen sink. Someday, I realized with sudden clarity, my youngest daughter is going to be a great pie-maker. All of a sudden, I felt warm and good. Imagine! A first-class pie-maker coming out of *my* womb! It could happen. Really, it could.

It wasn't until the next morning that I realized that it was time to give my youngest daughter my Tupperware dough-rolling sheet. I'd keep my rolling pin, though. Even I could handle Christmas cookies, and you never know when the spirit might move you.

Sex

The solution to all serious conflict is much easier than we've assumed: zero sex. It's guaranteed to wipe out the problem within one generation. Whatever the source of the trouble, simply target that group for mandatory zero sex.

I'm not being flippant. I am dead serious. It's not even an original idea. When there was conflict between the Jews and the Christians, and the Christians were in power, there were strict injunctions against sex for Jews, although, of course, it wasn't worded quite that way. For example, in 1750, Frederick II of Prussia issued a charter that divided all Jews into four groups. The "generally privileged" were accorded full residence and economic rights. The "regularly protected" meant the eldest Jewish son in a family inherited his father's rights of domicile and occupation. The "specially protected" were those Jews who had exceptional talents, such as outstanding writing ability. The "tolerated" were all other Jews. Tolerated Jews were not allowed to marry, which is just a polite way of saying zero sex. If you think this is an isolated instance, I suggest you read *Jewish People, Jewish Thought*,[19] by Robert M. Seltzer, which is where I first discovered this interesting information.

Of course (and in my opinion, thankfully) these early attempts at resolving conflict through zero sex were not totally successful. Fortunately, we've acquired more efficient and humane ways of providing for zero sex nowadays. Have you heard, for instance, the suggestion, currently being circulated in some areas of the United States, that any convicted sex-offender should be medically castrated? It's just a pill. Takes that sex drive right away, and boy, there's one deficiency that isn't going to be passed on anymore.

Zero sex may sound harsh, but that's only a matter of perspective. Roman Catholic nuns and priests have been doing it for centuries, although, I admit, that hasn't seemed to wipe them out, so maybe that's not such a good example. The Shakers, on the other hand, were pretty successful, and they were mostly lay folk. There are rumors that even Jesus adopted the zero sex policy, although there are also the Jesus/John rumors, which kind of puts a different light on the decision. If you find my mentioning such things offensive or even simply indiscreet, then not to worry. The solution is appallingly simple. Zero sex for writers. Banish that artistic gene. They'll be gone in a few generations, for sure.

Don't like big mouths? Zero sex. Hate liberals? Zero sex. "Liberals" is a dirty word now anyway. Want to eliminate welfare, poverty, the non-Caucasian race, the Irish IRA? Well, it's not as though nobody's ever mentioned the idea of zero sex before.

And speaking of the Jesus/John rumors, there's that whole gay/lesbian controversy now. Why, as I write I know of a Methodist minister who just got suspended because he performed a union ceremony for two individuals of the same gender. On the face of it, you'd think there wouldn't be any problem here, what with zero sex automatic in such situations, or at least zero offspring. There's the trouble, though. We've become so technologically advanced that all lesbians have to do today is to find a good sex donor and, what with intrauterine fertilization, even zero sex becomes problematic. If we aren't careful, we'll never eliminate such undesirables from our society, which, I suppose, is why that poor Methodist minister deserves to have half his congregation up in arms against him.

They've missed the point, though. Just say "no" to sex with ministers. That'd have tremendous side benefits as well. No more sex scandals among the clergy.

There is a downside to the zero sex solution, however, and I really believe we must be cognizant of it. It's these intellectuals who threaten to continue researching genetics. Why, already we're cloning sheep. Artificially replicated humans may only be a generation away, and then what good would zero

130

sex do! It's clear that we can't afford to waste time in this critical situation. It's because of those genetic scientists that the zero sex solution is endangered. We've got to get 'em. We've got to root 'em out of their laboratories, take away their tenure, and, above all else, slap the zero sex law on them. I'll help lobby the politicians. We've got to take action. Now!

Grace

A few years ago, on a visit to a California theological school, I came across a bumper sticker I loved immediately. "Grace Happens" it read. I put it on my car and enjoyed it immensely until the car finally wore out and some fellow who liked to tinker around with automobiles got a well-used message.

Grace Happens. Grace Happens? Well, maybe. Maybe it depends upon what kind of grace we're talking about. *Amazing grace, how sweet the sound that saved a wretch like me! I once was lost but now am found, was blind, but now I see.*[20] Is that the kind of grace that happens? The grace of the true believer? And if so, a true believer in what? God? And if so, what kind of God?

Does grace happen for those who have been taught, as many of us have been taught, to "cherish your doubts, for doubt is the attendant of truth?"

Somehow applauding the virtue of healthy skepticism just doesn't seem to match the sense of grace apparent in *T'was grace that taught my heart to fear, and grace my fears relieved; how precious did that grace appear the hour I first believed!* If grace happens, does it happen to you as frequently as it happens to everyone else?

I don't have a scholarly background on the nature of grace, nor do I have any statistical evidence for its existence or nonexistence. What I do have is a tiny experience of it, and what I have learned from that tiny experience of grace is this:

First, grace is authoritative. You don't question grace. If it happens, you know it, and you don't argue with it. Grace rules. It is supreme power; you surrender to it and it transforms you in the surrendering.

The first time I can recall ever experiencing grace was during what I now call my mid-life crisis. Sometimes I call it my faith crisis, but, unlike a mid-life crisis which ends when you get old enough, a faith crisis tends to wave on and on, hitting peaks now and then but never really becoming time-bound. So, during my mid-life crisis, I came home one day from my therapist having just been confronted with an unwanted, unexpected, and unsavory diagnosis. For the first time in my life, I recognized who I was, what I was. I didn't like it. How, I wondered, was I ever going to cope with this new understanding of myself. I was scared. I was hurting. I was sure I was going to fall completely apart. I was, literally, alone. Not one single thing had gone right that day and now I had this, this curse of a label crawling all over me.

I wanted someone, something to help me. I tried to pray to a God I wasn't sure I believed in. "God," I cried, "send me a sign. Let me know what I should do. Please. God, please." I'm not sure I am describing it accurately. Let's just say I was pretty desperate. I was also consumed with self-pity.

The God I've come to know has a great sense of timing and an even better sense of humor. In the midst of all my inner turmoil, I had a call of nature. I went into the bathroom, grunted around for a while, and then flushed the pot. That's when it happened. The toilet plugged up. The contents rose higher and higher. I couldn't control it. It was flooding over. It flooded over. All this yuk and mess all over the floor. It was horrid. Demoralizing. Disgusting. Degrading.

"Why, God? Why this, too! Why now, when I can hardly handle anything. Why now, in my hour of truth?" I started to cry. Then, suddenly I began to laugh. It was just that I had gotten such a concrete sign, as though God didn't trust me to understand anything more subtle. Shit happens. You gotta clean it up. Somehow, I managed to shut the water off and, right there in the midst of my hour of truth, I got down on my hands and knees and began to clean up the mess I had made.

I had my sign. I knew what I had to do. I had to clean up the mess my life was in, too. I knew it. I didn't question this truth. I didn't doubt. I surrendered to it. And, yes, even then I recognized it as the sign I had wanted. It wasn't until years later that I realized I had also experienced a small moment of grace. *Sovereign and transforming Grace, we invoke your quickening power; reign the spirit of this place, bless the purpose of this hour.*

The second truth which my experience has taught me about grace is that it only seems to work when it's dark. I mean that metaphorically, not literally, of course. You have to be suffering—dark—to experience grace. The old version said it, too. *Through many dangers, toils and snares, I have already come; 'tis grace that brought me safe thus far, and grace will lead me home.*

When I was doing the hospital part of my seminary training, I wrote a book of poem prayers which the hospital subsequently published. Writing this little book of poem-prayers meant a great deal to me. Never before had I been asked to put together any of my poems. I attended other people's poetry readings, not mine. My skills as a poet were pretty well ignored. My ability was unrecognized, unappreciated. It resided in the dark, along with a great deal of my creativity.

Then, one day, the Lutheran minister who was in charge of the pastoral care department at the hospital chanced to see a poem I had written about my experience. He subsequently contracted with me to write this little book. It was incredible. He not only wanted me to use my talents, he offered to pay me as well! His was an action of caring, of love, of generosity, of faith. For me, his confidence in me, his affirmation of me, was a moment of grace.

Jim Marshall. That's what I'll call the minister who paved the way for this moment of grace. Jim Marshall, highly regarded by colleagues and lay persons alike, left a trail of such kindnesses wherever he went. Eventually, his skill and caring took him away, to a larger city. One day, in this new city, the Rev. Dr. Jim Marshall poured a flammable substance over himself and set himself on fire. I don't know why. I don't know any of the details. I don't know what demons he fought, what sorrows he experienced, what caused him to finally abandon hope, or to feel that hope had abandoned him to the dark. Yet, to the day I die, I will never look at this small collection of poems which he helped me publish without thinking of him with love and without hoping that somehow, wherever he is now, he, too, is experiencing a moment of grace. *Holy and creative Light, we invoke your kindling ray; draw upon our spirit's night, as the darkness turns to day.*

The third and final truth I have gleaned about grace is that, together, we can create an environment which will foster the experience for others. This environment is called community. I'd like to describe one incident where I recently saw community in action such that it brought about an atmosphere where grace happened. It was the second Sunday in October. An African-American minister of my acquaintance had invited me to attend his service. Promptly at 10:30 a.m., Dan and I arrived at the Mount Moriah Missionary Baptist Church in North Omaha—right in the heart of Omaha's black community. We left the church at 2 p.m.

Ten thirty. Eleven thirty. Twelve thirty. One thirty. Two. That's three and a half hours of black Baptist revival. It was the first time I had ever experienced a Baptist service, the first time I had ever attended an all-black church. It was interesting, to say the least. It was powerful. It was also, above all else, warm and inviting. I can't help telling you that I felt a little like the lonely rich white couple in one of Maya Angelou's stories who wound up begging their maid to let them watch, just watch, her and her friends having fun at one of their weekend gatherings.

There was a sense of community in this historic old Baptist church which I have rarely experienced and which I can't help envying, for I have never felt it in such abundance, sad to say, in any other churches. There was an openness and a personal welcome that, quite frankly, many congregations would do well to emulate. I can sum up the service best, perhaps, by relating one small vignette.

It was toward the end of the morning, no, early afternoon, worship—the time described in the order of service as an "Invitation to Christian Discipleship." Among the half dozen or so individuals who had decided to make a public commitment to this faith and this church, was a somewhat disheveled man, thirtyish, wearing an old white sweatshirt, missing two front teeth. He gave the appearance of being down and out. He was last in line to be received into this community and when his turn came to share his reasons for being there he said, earnestly and simply,

"I am not a good man. But I am trying to change."

For just a moment in that church where interactive participation is a loud constant, there was total silence.

"I am not a good man. But I am trying to change."

What kind of community can create a climate where an individual feels safe enough to make a confession like that? It is, I believe, a community that says, as this one literally did to that troubled individual, "We accept you just as you are." It's a community that says, as this one did, "If you will let us, we will be with you as you change." It's a community that can fill the anxious soul with hope and stir the dull and hardened heart with a longing and a love. Such is the power of grace.

In this last half-century traditional churches have witnessed a rebellion against the restraints, dogma, and hypocrisy that so often seem to accompany organized religion. Some preachers have responded by systematically ridding themselves and their congregations of "outdated" spiritual language and practice. My mother attended one of the very first worship services I ever conducted. I wasn't even in seminary yet. Afterwards, she said it was a nice sermon and that she had enjoyed it and that I had done a great job, etc. In other words, she said all the right things. Then her face took on a troubled, puzzled note.

"There wasn't any place for prayer in it, though," she murmured.

You know, I hadn't even missed it. That's how far removed I was from the possibilities of prayer.

I think it's like that with grace, too. Grace enriches the soul. It forgives and redeems. It fills the anxious soul with hope and stirs the dull heart with a longing and a love. Is there a place for grace in our congregations, in our lives? If not, I say we'd do well to create such a place. Grace happens. May we be open to it, now and forever. *To the anxious soul impart hope, all other hopes above; stir the dull and hardened heart with a longing and a love.* Amen

Deathing

Uncle dies.

I finish scraping a carrot for tonight's stew, stick it under running water and shake it off. It alters nothing, this carrot. Uncle dies in spite of the carrot, in spite of my scraping the carrot. He dies this very moment, or, rather, these moments, for I have read somewhere that it takes about twelve minutes for the organ functions to cease. Even longer for the hair to die. Maybe a day. Maybe it takes a month, for the hair. Briefly, I study the clock over my kitchen sink, then I pick up another carrot.

For one year we have anticipated this event. Uncle's wife, daughter, son, everybody knew, or at least strongly suspected, from the day of his first surgery, which was not altogether successful. "Uncle," I said, "you are dying," though in truth the words were "You're looking good. Have you started

chemo yet?" I paraded my children in front of him, and we all posed together in front of several cameras. One of the cameras was a Polaroid. Carefully, elaborately, we examined the pictures. Aunt gave me a print, which I brought home and stuck on the refrigerator under a clothespin magnet one of the kids had given me as some Mother's Day gift.

I clean another carrot. Angrily I shove the peels down the disposal and turn the water on full blast. My hand is shaking. I am so angry I could take my hand and throw it down the disposal as well, but I don't, for I know I will need it. I, after all, am not dying. Uncle dies, not I. Twelve minutes, I tell myself. It will be over in twelve minutes. Less, now.

I was only five when I first discovered dying. My dog Benny got hit by a car. He yipped, but then his tongue grew dry and his legs began to stiffen. His body quivered, then wouldn't move at all. His eyesight faded, his hearing went out…. I didn't understand. I cried for hours, until my mother soothed me finally by allowing me to paint my fingernails with her flamingo red polish.

Uncle's anger is fading fast. Perhaps it is because he has experienced so much pain. Pain compromises anger. Uncle feels pain so intense that it is greater than anything previous, greater even than when the morphine no longer worked. The pain knots his middle; he is nauseated, breathless. Beads of sweat appear from nowhere on his head. I have wondered about this. In my reading I do not recall anything about the sweat, not when the patient is in a coma anyway. I presume Uncle is in a coma, though, of course, I cannot verify that detail until later.

Uncle is something of a stranger to me. We lived far apart when I was growing up, so that I saw him only on short vacations. I remember once he took me and my cousins to the beach. He wore a shirt with gaudy Hawaiian flowers on it and he sat all day under a huge umbrella, reading. He never seemed to know what to say to me, or perhaps he just didn't care enough to try. Probably he was too tired. He wasn't a blood relative, anyway. Correction. He *isn't* a blood relative. It's not over yet.

I glance at the clock again, but it is a defiant gesture only. Already I have lost track of time. I try to ignore Uncle. I reach for another carrot, but my arm refuses to cooperate. I stare at the carrot, willing my hand to pick it up. It's no good, though. It's never any good to fight the deathing experience.

Poor Uncle. The numbness has settled in. He tries to speak. He has something he wants to say to Aunt. Something important. Something he forgot to tell her. He does not know if Aunt is beside him anymore. She held his hand, and cried a little. She was there a little while ago. He tries to lift his head to search for Aunt. Uncle's head won't move. He opens his eyes. Panic overwhelms him. He opens his eyes, but nothing is there. "No," he tries to say. "Not yet, please, not yet."

I remember once when a little girl was drowning. She was a total stranger, that one. For her, the pain came from the water. Water everywhere, inside and out, and when she tried to speak, water spat out in wordless cries.

Oh, Uncle, it is devastating, this blackness. Out my kitchen window, where moments ago my children were playing happily in snow, white snow, there is now dark. Carrots, orange, have vanished, though my eyes gaze at them feverishly. Fear not the darkness, Uncle, for at the end of the tunnel is….

Uncle believes. Always it is the same. And always the belief comes with the darkness. Strange! What gene in us has programmed such a response? Listen to me, Uncle, I tell you we are but fancy 1's and 0's, programmed from the instant we breathe air. Tick, tock, tick, tock, 1, 0, 1, 0, the years grind by, filled with joys and sorrows and gaudy flower swim trunks on sun stroked beaches and little known relatives from distant cities who dash in and out, barely saying hello before they say goodbye again and who know nothing at all about you, and also everything. Dear, dear Uncle. I wonder what time it is. My kitchen clock ticks loudly, but I cannot hear it.

The swirling approaches, first distant, then nearer and nearer. Uncle feels it, senses its magnetic pull. Swirling is an inadequate word, but it is hard to describe otherwise. It is like the fetus passing through the vaginal canal. Yes, I remember now. But it's hard to describe nonetheless. It must be experienced, this swirling. And then the warmth. Warmth. That is Uncle's final sensation.

My face is flushed as I pick up the last of the carrots. I wipe perspiration from my forehead with the back of my hand. Quickly, I glance out the window. My son is sledding down the hill. He turns at the foot of the hill, looks toward the house and my window. I wave at him and select some potatoes for the stew. Carefully, I rinse them off. I take my peeler and begin to unwind tiny curls of brown. Tonight, I think. Tonight Aunt will call with the news.

"Oh, Aunt," I will say. "Oh, Aunt, I am sorry."

Conversions

One of my colleagues presented a paper not long ago at the theology section of a conference I attended. In it, he contended that the apostle Paul had undergone a major grieving experience and that the episode on the road to Damascus was what mental health experts of today would call a conversion disorder. His study was interesting, his presentation polished, and his manner engaging. Generally speaking, too much theology in too short a time-span tends to leave me feeling as run over as if I'd been in a Looney Tune, but I'd had absolutely none of this flattened out response during his talk. Yet, something…something was troubling me. Suddenly, I knew!

Why, I'd had one of those things he was calling a disorder! Oh, all right, it wasn't exactly like what had happened to Paul back there in Biblical days, but it had certainly changed my life good and well. And, while there had been a considerable element of disorder to the whole experience, and while the term "conversion" might in some ways be descriptive enough, I darn well wasn't happy to hear it labeled a "disorder." No, sir-ee, not even if the mental health experts did call it that, why, it was positively medieval to label it that way, sort of like calling the mentally distressed "mad." Naturally, I managed to convey this sentiment to my colleague during the question/answer period immediately following his talk. His response was unoriginal. He simply pointed out that it wasn't his label; it was that of the experts, and they should know.

I mumbled something about how they should know *better*, and how he should challenge the use of such negative terminology, not perpetuate it. I suspect he thought I was being *defensive*. Now, there's a term even I can admit to—on rare occasions, of course. I also suspect that he, my colleague, had never had one of those conversion experiences, or he would have been less enthusiastic about designating it a disorder.

Something good inevitably comes out of even such blatant evil as someone disagreeing with me, and, in this instance, my colleague's comments set me to thinking about the nature of conversions. I decided that conversions are the penultimate "zero" experience. They're…

sighting freedom from behind bars,

coming close to danger and surviving,

bridging the invisible,

driving into another era,

accomplishing the impossible,

emerging from a black hole as something unexpected,

climbing Jacob's ladder to an opening in the sky,

experiencing religion in a totally new way,

but they are nothing, no absolutely *nothing* like a disorder. I'm sorry, mental health experts, but that pathetic pretense of a metaphor just simply misses the essence of conversions.

Creation

First, there is nothing. Zero. Naught. Null. Non-being. Non-existence, non-entity, absence, darkness, emptiness, hollowness, blankness, oblivion, void, vacuum, vacuity, vacancy. Then there is something. Non-zero. Being, life, existence, presence, light, fullness, anything, an idea, a thought, a product, the world, the word. In-between nothing and something is creation.

Creation seems to be a process which turns zero into non-zero, but the nature of that process remains a source of mystery and awe. Some things foster creation: periods of quiet reflection, intellectual or emotional or sensual stimulus, competition, struggle, need, sex. Even something so unoriginal as a deadline can be yeast for originality. Today we've become so familiar with the act of creativity that it's surprising we haven't trivialized it, but we haven't. The act of giving birth to a child, for instance, is one of the most routine acts of creativity we experience, occurring (in the United States) roughly once every eight seconds, yet its frequent repetition has done nothing to delete the awe and amazement that accompanies each birth.

There is something essentially *clever* about creation. When I was in Las Vegas recently, I was awed and amazed by the elaborate flashing lights, the ingenious public displays, the immediacy of the slot machines even in the airports, etc. I was so awed, in fact, that after one weekend I could hardly wait to leave, which just goes to show that maybe even creation can be overdone. Nonetheless, I couldn't help appreciating the sheer cleverness of those who lived and worked in this "city of sin." I suppose it's a little like you have to appreciate the cleverness of the Devil. Anyway, I chuckled over one hotel's marquee in particular. The vacancy sign was lit up in bright red—a clear sign of the zero experience. Not to worry, though, for, in even bigger letters was the reassuring note that this hotel was "HIGHLY RECOMMENDED— BY OWNER."

Clever, I thought, chuckling. Inventive. Creative. I found myself hoping that the owner would have success with this sign. Such creativity, it seemed to me, deserved success.

As I've reflected on the impact of this sign of creativity (a very literal one, I might add), it occurs to me to wonder about the experience God has had in creating this world. In the beginning the world was without form and void. God's spirit had a vacancy—room for something. With considerable cleverness, to say nothing of speed, God created day, night, heaven, earth, and all the creatures of the earth, including us. I like to think that this world as we know it (another very literal sign of creativity) comes highly recommended, by owner. Surely such creativity deserves success.

Of course, there's the catch. Leaving aside questions of omnipotence, but opening up issues of free will, it appears to me that we humans play a significant part in the ultimate "success" of this creative venture. What happens because of our presence here? Will spiritual visitors to this world think creation has been overdone and want to leave after a long weekend? Or will they want to stay on because they sense it will be a wonderful experience, filled with growth, love, joy, and, perhaps best of all, humor?

What we do matters. In fact, what we do helps create the creation. The creator and the created do not exist in isolation one from the other. Zero is firmly embedded within non-zero. It just takes a little imagination, and a lot of faith, to see it.

Endnotes

162

1. This passage and all quotations in this section on the Tarot are taken from *Yeats, the Tarot, and the Golden Dawn* (Dublin: Dolmen Press, 1982) by Liam Miller.

2. "Richard Young Memorial Universe," by Sarah Voss, appeared first in *The Porcelain Toad*, Spring, 1989. Used with permission.

3. From *Singing, Laughing, Weeping, Praying,* by Sarah Voss, publication pending.

4. Statistics cited here are taken from *Fifty Simple Things You Can Do to Save the Earth*, Berkeley, CA: Earthworks Press, 1989.

5. See Robert Ornstein and Paul Ehrlich, *New World, New Mind*, New York: Simon and Schuster, 1989.

6. Robert Fulghum, *All I Really Need to Know I Learned in Kindergarten*, New York: Ballantine,1993.

7. Donella H. Meadows, *The Sun* 231 (March, 1995),13.

8. These findings were reported in the *Menninger Letter*, 3:9 (September, 1995) and 3:7 (July, 1995).

9. *Menninger Letter*, 3:7 (July 1995).

10. *Newsweek*, March, 1996.

11. *University of Nebraska, Omaha, (UNO) Gateway*, March, 1996.

12. *Science News,* 147 (February 25, 1995).

13. *Wall Street Journal*, July, 1994.

14. Mark Hartwig, *Focus on the Family Citizen* (June 21, 1993).

15. *Focus on Family Citizen*, June, 1993.

16. Edward MacNeal, *Mathsemantics*, New York: Viking, 1994.

17. The capital of Burma is Rangoon, probably founded in the sixth century, and until the eighteenth century a small fishing village. It was named capital in 1753.

18. Jack Canfield and Mark Victor Hansen, *Chicken Soup for the Soul*, Deerfield Beach, FL: Health Communications, 1993.

19. Robert Seltzer, *Jewish People, Jewish Thought*, New York: Macmillan Publishing Co. 1980.

20. Lines appearing in italic are verses from *Amazing Grace*, by John Newton, and *Sovereign and Transforming Grace*, by Frederick Henry Hedge.

163

About the Photos

1. Nothing: The pig was spotted doing what pigs do on a farm in rural Iowa.
2. Evil: A variation on an old theme. The women posed for this in Omaha, Nebraska before the story was even conceived.
3. Blackout: Omaha at night.
4. Thanks: The billboard was an advertisement for well-known Omaha attorney Ron Palagi.
5. Ghosts: Assembled from items found on a restaurant table and in the photographer's imagination.
6. Compassion: Sunset in Memorial Park, Omaha.
7. Words: Performing mime at Sea World, Orlando, Florida.
8. Profanity: Sign spotted in a restaurant in Neligh, Nebraska.
9. Games: The chess set was handmade of plumbing parts. The second photo

is of an unidentified experimenter at the Epcot Center, Orlando, Florida.

10. Olive: Highway sign near Kearney, Nebraska.

11. Stones: In order, these include author near Eyeries, Ireland, Carhenge Sculpture Park near Alliance, Nebraska, and a clever snow sculpture spotted in Memorial Park, Omaha.

12. Home: Scene from Las Vegas, Nevada.

13. Dialogue: Sign in Dodge Park, Omaha, Nebraska following rains in 1997.

14. Choice: Dublin, Ireland.

15. Probability: Sunflower seeds, discovered at Farmers' Market in downtown Omaha, Nebraska.

16. Fences: Barbed wire coiled alongside road in Valentine, Nebraska.

17. Singing: Melinda, no longer thirteen, but still singing.

18. Rainbows: From the air somewhere over Puerto Rico on a perfectly clear day.

19. Apple Pie: Look closely—the pie is store-bought.

20. Sex: Bumper sticker first spotted in Omaha, Nebraska.

21. Grace: College professor attending seminar at the University of Nebraska, Omaha, where the photographer teaches biochemistry.

22. Deathing: Road signs marking the place where three individuals were the victims of fatal automobile accidents near Burton, Nebraska.

23. Conversions: *The window was once the source of air for slaves at Fort Christian, at Charlotte Amalie, Virgin Islands. *The geyser is at

Yellowstone National Park. *The bridge was taken on a foggy morning at Levi Carter Park in Omaha. *Street scene from Omaha. *Old, heavy piece of steel water pipe in photographer's backyard. Used variously as an incinerator (before the city laws prohibited such), a children's sand box (before the author knew it had once been an incinerator), and a planter (which never did work very well, hence the author's desire to get rid of it). Removed by photographer, with effort. *Mushroom growing in old silver maple tree. *View from inside Crossroads Shopping Mall, Omaha. *Manger scene with candles, North Omaha, Nebraska.

24. Creation: Two views of the same sign. Las Vegas, Nevada.